# Own Your Psychology Major!

# Own Your Psychology Major!

## A Guide to Student Success

**Glenn Geher**

 AMERICAN PSYCHOLOGICAL ASSOCIATION

Washington, DC

Published by
American Psychological Association
750 First Street, NE
Washington, DC 20002
www.apa.org

APA Order Department
P.O. Box 92984
Washington, DC 20090-2984
Phone: (800) 374-2721; Direct: (202) 336-5510
Fax: (202) 336-5502; TDD/TTY: (202) 336-6123
Online: http://www.apa.org/pubs/books
E-mail: order@apa.org

In the U.K., Europe, Africa, and the Middle East, copies may be ordered from
Eurospan Group
c/o Turpin Distribution
Pegasus Drive
Stratton Business Park
Biggleswade, Bedfordshire
SG18 8TQ United Kingdom
Phone: +44 (0) 1767 604972
Fax: +44 (0) 1767 601640
Online: https://www.eurospanbookstore.com/apa
E-mail: eurospan@turpin-distribution.com

Typeset in Meridien by Circle Graphics, Inc., Reisterstown, MD

Printer: Sheridan Books, Chelsea, MI
Cover Designer: Gwen J. Grafft, Minneapolis, MN

**Library of Congress Cataloging-in-Publication Data**
Names: Geher, Glenn, author.
Title: Own your psychology major! : a guide to student success / by Glenn Geher.
Description: Washington, DC : American Psychological Association, [2019] |
   Includes bibliographical references and index.
Identifiers: LCCN 2018044231 (print) | LCCN 2018046865 (ebook) | ISBN 9781433830723
   (eBook) | ISBN 1433830728 (eBook) | ISBN 9781433830662
   (pbk.) | ISBN 1433830663 (pbk.)
Subjects: LCSH: Psychology—Handbooks, manuals, etc.
Classification: LCC BF131 (ebook) | LCC BF131 .G374 2019 (print) |
   DDC 150—dc23
LC record available at https://lccn.loc.gov/2018044231

**British Library Cataloguing-in-Publication Data**
A CIP record is available from the British Library.

*Printed in the United States of America*

http://dx.doi.org/10.1037/0000127-000

10 9 8 7 6 5 4 3 2 1

*For Kathy, who shines bright light on everything,
and for Megan and Andrew, who are among the leaders
of the next generation.*

# Contents

## I

*Ethical and Social Responsibility: How to Use Psychology to Make the World a Better Place* 1

## II

*Knowledge Base: The Content of Psychology* 23

## III

*Scientific Inquiry and Critical Thinking* 59

# IV

# V

# Preface: A Note for Advisors and Instructors

As department chair of psychology at the State University of New York (SUNY) New Paltz for 8 years (between 2009 and 2017), I had the privilege of facilitating the success of hundreds of psychology students with all kinds of interests and goals. On the basis of the American Psychology Association's (APA's; 2013) *APA Guidelines for the Undergraduate Psychology Major* (see https://www.apa.org/ed/precollege/about/undergraduate-major.aspx), the psychology major at New Paltz is a strong program, providing students with experiences with research, statistics, internships, and advanced writing opportunities both inside and outside of the classroom. Armed with a powerful set of intellectual skills, students who seize the opportunities that are offered and who choose to make the most out of their academic experiences have extraordinary potential to thrive. Those who graduate with our major in psychology consistently succeed—in getting into applied graduate programs (e.g., master's programs in mental health counseling), doctoral programs (e.g., PhD programs in quantitative psychology), and health-related careers; finding jobs related to industry; landing great internship opportunities across the globe; and more.

A primary focus of my work over the years has been to interact directly with hundreds of students each semester to help them understand what the psychology major is designed to do and what they can do to ensure their success during their 4 years in college—and beyond. *Own Your Psychology Major! A Guide to Student Success* is designed to provide this kind of motivational and practical guidance to a broad audience, including psychology students (or potential psychology students) from across the globe. The audience for this book also includes individuals who surround psychology students, such as parents, advisors, and professors. It is my hope that all who have a vested interest in a psychology student's success will find this book useful.

Further, to help students connect with the *APA Guidelines* that are likely shaping their educational experiences in important ways, this book is organized according to the structure of the *Guidelines*, and it works to demystify this structure so that students can understand and appreciate why the curriculum is designed as it is.

Psychology continues to be a popular major at schools across the United States and in similar countries. My psychology department includes more than 500 psychology majors at any given time; this is about 8% of all students at the university. And this pattern is quite representative of schools across the land (see Clay, 2017). This popularity associated with the psychology major is interesting given that many people do not see psychology as having the same practical value and real-world applicability as, say, engineering. That said, this book demonstrates how a solid education in psychology provides students with a variety of highly marketable skills. Further, there are various industries, such as the modern mental health industry, that actively seek employees with a background in psychology.

On my *Psychology Today* blog (https://www.psychologytoday.com/us/blog/darwins-subterranean-world), I post frequently about issues related to cultivating student success in psychology majors. The reader feedback I receive from such posts (often in the form of comments on the post itself) tends to fall within a few predictable themes: (a) gratitude for helping show what the psychology major is like from the inside, (b) a new understanding of the breadth of the field of psychology, and (c) a newfound appreciation for the scientific process that underlies the field. These comments, along with the feedback I get from recent graduates from my institution, confirmed to me that there needs to be a higher level of *metalearning* going on in psychology. Why am I learning what I'm learning? How does my new knowledge relate to real-world problems? What skills can I now apply to solve those problem? These are the questions I hope to answer in this book, as they relate to the psychology undergraduate course of study.

One thing that my students regularly comment on regarding my work is this: *I care about them, and they know it and appreciate it*. This book represents my genuine interest in helping a broader group of students take the necessary steps to succeed as psychology students. Think of it as something of a guidebook for this intellectual journey.

# Acknowledgments

Having taught and guided undergraduate psychology students since 1994, I cannot overstate how thrilled I am to have been given the opportunity to write this book.

I owe a huge debt of gratitude to the thousands of students I've gotten to know over the years. Since the first day I taught Introduction to Psychology in Conant Hall at the University of New Hampshire (UNH), I've been blessed to have worked with students who have inspired and amazed me on a daily basis. From teaching and mentoring students at UNH, Bowdoin College, Western Oregon University, Husson College, Florida Atlantic University, Chongqing University of Education, and, my home of nearly 2 decades, SUNY New Paltz, I have been nothing short of privileged. Watching my students over the years grow into leaders in all kinds of capacities is the primary reward of my work. In this profession, as I tell my students regularly, *your success is my success*. Although there are all kinds of reasons to be concerned about the future of the world right now, knowing that there are so many bright, active, forward-thinking, and capable members of the next generation gives me reason for all kinds of optimism.

I want to give a shout-out to the teachers who have influenced me over the years. Like so many of us, I have had dozens of great teachers who have shaped my approach to pretty much everything. Here, I acknowledge five particular teachers who have inspired and influenced me most across my own education. In high school, I was fortunate to wrestle under the tutelage of Coach Ed Gibbons. If there is anyone in the world who can make someone believe in himself or herself, it's Coach Gibbons. In college, I was extremely fortunate to work on research under the mentorship of Dr. Benjamin Sachs at the University of Connecticut. Dr. Sachs taught me many things, including the fact that evolution touches everything. My mentor in graduate school, Dr. Becky Warner, influenced me in so many ways—not only teaching me about statistics and research methods but also, in an understated way, modeling such virtues as respect, open-mindedness, and self-reliance. I could not have had a better mentor in graduate school.

I also have to acknowledge my informal postdoctoral advisor, Dr. Gordon Gallup of the University at Albany. Although I never formally worked under Gordon, I have gotten to know him quite well over the years. He is one of the most highly published scholars in the history of psychology. Yet he is one of the most down-to-earth people there is. He has always impressed me because he cares more about supporting his students and alumni than he does about getting out the next publication. He is a model citizen and an inspiration. I also would be remiss to not acknowledge the influence of my good friend (and fellow professor) Peter Kaufman. Peter, a sociologist and an award-winning teacher, has cultivated an approach to teaching that is famous for including compassion and a true appreciation for what each and every student brings to the table. Talking with Peter about teaching over the years has added greatly to my own work in this regard, and I deeply appreciate the influence that he has had on what goes on in my classroom.

Each of these teachers has, in one way or another, shaped the ideas found within the pages of this book. Here's to hoping that the product inspires the next generation in all kinds of positive ways.

Last but not least, I thank the American Psychological Association (APA) for giving me this opportunity. APA is, in many ways, where the buck stops on a global scale when it comes to psychology, and I see it as an enormous honor to have worked with APA on this project. Senior acquisitions editor Linda Malnasi McCarter and on-the-ground editor Susan Herman have been exemplary to work with on this project: constructive, diligent, and visionary. And special thanks to Liz Brace and Elizabeth Budd for all of their detailed work in carrying this book into production and across the finish line!

# A Note to Students

Psychology is a hugely popular major, and careers related to psychology are growing—so now is a good time to be majoring in psychology. This book is designed as something of a guidebook for psychology students who really want to get the most out of their education. If you want to have an exceptional college experience and want to make sure to set yourself up on a path toward success, then this book is for you.

## What Is the Point of This Book?

Psychology is famous for not being what people initially think it is. As you'll see throughout this book, it is common for students to go into psychology thinking that the field is primarily focused on various forms of psychological abnormalities and therapeutic approaches. As any student of psychology comes to find out, these facets of the field represent only a sliver of what is in store for you in this major. This book will help provide you with a large-scale perspective of the field as well as guidance on many specific activities that you can take part in to ensure that you are getting the most out of your experience with the major. My specific goals in writing this book include the following:

- help you to see the breadth of content in the field of psychology,
- demonstrate the scientific tools that psychologists use,
- give you a heads-up about some of the large questions that underlie the field of psychology,

---

*Note.* Sections of several chapters in this book were adapted from various blog posts of mine from *Psychology Today* ("Darwin's Subterranean World"). American Psychological Association owns copyright to all content in this book, and I own copyright to the material as it appears on my blog posts. Any lists, infographics, tables, and other content from either source may be reproduced for personal use only.

- show you how to make the most of the research process,
- offer you tips on how to take advantage of internship opportunities,
- provide clear and specific guidance regarding graduate programs related to psychology,
- provide clear and specific guidance regarding careers related to psychology, and
- help you get a sense of how an education in psychology can lead you to make the world a better place.

Throughout this book, I'll be clueing you in to the main content and skill areas that your undergraduate psychology degree will most likely require. Odds are, you didn't know just how much ground your psychology major would cover—and that's OK. I've taught undergraduates since 1994, and I have more than a hunch that most students don't know exactly what they're getting into when they declare themselves psychology majors.

As I'm laying out the content and skills that a typical psychology BS or BA degree track entails, I'll try to help you see how these areas are all related to each other. More than that, I'll help you see how they are related to the knowledge and skills that today's psychology professionals have said they want new graduates to bring to the field. You may already know that the largest organization of psychology professionals in the United States is the American Psychological Association (APA). It's the hope and aspiration of APA members that have shaped the foundation of the curriculum your professors are using today. Leaders of undergraduate psychology programs across the U.S. look to the *APA Guidelines for the Undergraduate Psychology Major* (2013). The *Guidelines*, as well as psychology course requirements nationwide, are updated regularly based on trends that APA member researchers and practitioners identify through their work.

The 2013 iteration of the *Guidelines*, which is the most recently updated version, breaks the subject matter into five goals, which I cover in this book over 12 short chapters. I also include a host of examples that will help you form pictures in your mind of what lies ahead. I hope that by understanding the five goals and seeing some examples of what it looks like to practice them both inside and outside the classroom, you'll be excited and proud of your major. My other hope is that you'll be inspired to make choices that take you beyond *This is required, so I'll do it* and, instead, adopt a mind-set of *These are my goals and I'm going to achieve them!*

OK, ready? Here we go!

# ETHICAL AND SOCIAL RESPONSIBILITY: HOW TO USE PSYCHOLOGY TO MAKE THE WORLD A BETTER PLACE

1

Any academic institution that is worth its weight makes ethical and social responsibility an important part of its educational approach. As you look over the courses that are part of your psychology major, make a mental note of how many course titles or course descriptions mention ethics and social responsibility. Even if those exact words aren't used, it is likely that these themes will come up in one form or another. That's because, in recent decades, the professions that many psychology majors enter—such as education, business, and health care—have been calling on colleges to teach ethics, values, and personal and social responsibility (Schneider & Hersh, 2005).

The American Psychological Association (APA) defined a set of five learning goals that play a major role in shaping undergraduate psychology major programs across the United States. As you will see, while these goals include the standard intellectual outcomes, such as knowledge and critical thinking skills, they also include *Ethical and Social Responsibility in a Diverse World*. Thus, embedded into an APA-influenced psychology program are elements designed to get students to think about the broader world and their place in it.

## Chapter 1: What the Pros Hope You Will Learn in Your Psychology Major: Five Goals From the *APA Guidelines for the Undergraduate Psychology Major*

Chapter 1 describes the five basic APA goals used to shape undergraduate major programs and highlights how these goals are designed to help build knowledgeable, thoughtful, and ethical leaders for the future of the behavioral sciences.

## Chapter 2: Making a Difference: How the Psychology Curriculum Cultivates Ethical and Socially Responsible Leadership

At the end of the day, a strong psychology graduate will typically succeed and ultimately attain a career related to the field. But as citizens of this planet, we might want to strive for more than just getting a good job in our field. We might be interested in taking steps to make this world a better place. As it happens, a psychology education provides many skills that can be used to make this world a better place. Chapter 2 is dedicated to the various ways that psychology research and applied psychology (such as mental health counseling) can be used to make a positive difference in the world.

# What the Pros Hope You Will Learn in Your Psychology Major
## Five Goals From the *APA Guidelines for the Undergraduate Psychology Major*

1

I signed up for Introductory Psychology in the fall of my freshman year—1988. I was at the University of Connecticut, or UCONN as it's known. UCONN is a pretty large university, and, as such, there were hundreds of people in this class. I remember it like it was yesterday. It was a morning class—9:30 a.m. No problem. I was there with my notebook and pen, feeling bright and cheery. This was going to be it—the class that would inspire me and shape my next 60 or so years.

The professor emerged at the front of the room. She seemed to be nearly 40 and seemed quite professorly. She had glasses and was dressed very properly. And she spoke exactly as I figured a professor would speak. She sounded like a genius!

After some basic introductions about herself and the class, she turned on the overhead projector to show some transparency slides on the screen. This was *the* cutting-edge technology in 1988. I decided that I was going to take notes like a demon, writing down every single thing that she put up on screen. Here we go!

Slide 1 came up, with the title "The Chemical Properties of Neural Transmission." *Wait a minute!* I thought. *Was I in the right class? Look at all those chemical symbols up there! I did not like chemistry in high school! Why is this psychology professor teaching us about chemistry!? Ack!!!*

http://dx.doi.org/10.1037/0000127-001
*Own Your Psychology Major! A Guide to Student Success*, by G. Geher

Slide 2 was called "The Electrophysiology of Neural Transmission." *Oh no—it gets worse! Voltages? Negative and positive symbols? Potassium? What in the world was this lady talking about?! What does this have to do with psychology?*

I left after that first lecture totally shaken. I don't want to study this stuff! After all, isn't psychology all about therapy and counseling?

Two days later, I went back to that class determined not to be discouraged. *It would have to get better—things could only improve, right?* I sat down and opened up my notebook. I waited in anticipation as the professor turned on that transparency projector. Believe it or not, it did get worse. Today's lesson was on statistics. *Now she's really done it*, I thought. *Greek symbols? Equations? Square root? What in the world?*

Well guess what? The esteemed Professor Gustafson was, in fact, teaching psychology, and masterfully at that. The problem was, I didn't realize then that the field of psychology is not by any means synonymous with counseling or psychotherapy. Psychology is much bigger than that.

At the time, UCONN actually had split Introduction to Psychology into Parts 1 and 2. And we didn't get to issues related to therapy until well into the second semester! By the time we got to that subject, I actually had my mind set on psychological research—something that I didn't even know existed when I first walked onto the campus when I started my freshman year.

I tell this story partly to let you know early on what I didn't know upfront: Psychology has many subfields. Most of these subfields are strictly scientific and research based. Further, the non–research-based parts of psychology include much more than just the area of psychotherapy. When I was 18 years old, I had no idea about any of this!

## Let Me Introduce Myself

This book is designed as a guidebook, with me as your guide. As such, I hope you'll allow me a page or two to introduce myself.

As already mentioned, I decided not too long after plunging into my psychology major that I wanted to do research. I soon concluded, however, that I did not want to work with rats as part of my research. Here's why. I had enjoyed Dr. Sachs's Animal Behavior class and asked if I could join his research lab after the semester was over. I didn't know much about his lab, but I figured that under his mentorship, it'd be a great experience. After a pretty intensive interview, he took me in! And I got to help with all kinds of great research on mating behaviors in rats. One thing I learned along the way was this: Female rats will only be open to mating if they are at their peak of ovulation, so if you study mating behavior in rats, you likely will find yourself having to give the females shots of hormones to facilitate ovulation. Well, let's just say that I got bitten pretty badly when it was my turn to give the rat a shot. I was bleeding profusely—it was a mess!

This experience pretty much shaped my future, actually. I didn't enjoy working with rats, but I liked the "hard science" way of thinking that went along with research. So I ended up applying to a PhD program in human social psychology at the University of New Hampshire (UNH). I figured that humans are animals too. I was thrilled to be in a PhD program—and do you know that they waived all of my tuition? They even paid me a stipend of about $10,000 a year in living expenses for 5 years. Turns out, this is standard practice for many PhD programs. Just something to keep in mind!

Anyway, I ended up doing alright in graduate school—getting my PhD in 5 years, getting a solid publication along the way, and meeting my lovely wife, Kathy, who started the same program in my same cohort (meaning in the same group at the same time).

For me, the best part of my PhD program at UNH was the focus on college teaching. Did you know that most college professors have zero education on the teaching process? It's true. But in the psychology department at UNH, they not only have their graduate students teach, they also have them take a yearlong class on college teaching. That experience made things clear for me: After starting out as a ho-hum student during my freshman and sophomore years of college, I truly, at the end of the day, came to love college teaching. These days I can connect with students across the spectrum of motivational levels. In fact, I love the challenge of working with students who are apathetic and who goof off!

Anyway, I finished my PhD in social psychology in 1997 and found a tenure-track job at Western Oregon University. I worked there for 2 years, and it was a great experience, even with the heavy teaching load—12 classes a year at the time.

I have been a member of the psychology department at the State University of New York (SUNY) New Paltz since 2000. I teach classes, run a lab, and even served as department chair for several years. I love meeting with individual students to provide them guidance regarding what classes to take, whether to do an internship, how to get involved in research, what extracurricular activities to join, and so on. Mentoring psychology students at every single step of the journey is my passion, so I'm thrilled to have this opportunity to help guide *you* in a similar way.

# So, What Is Psychology?

Psychology is the field of inquiry dealing with behavior and psychological processes (such as cognitive, emotional, and motivational processes) across all animal species. By *field of inquiry*, I mean that it's a body of knowledge on a particular topic that essentially wants to keep growing. There is no particular psychology course that will, in and of itself, teach you everything about human behavior. People who practice in the field are constantly asking questions, pushing ahead and out to the margins to find out more. And as a student, you'll be expected to participate in the inquiry process too.

This scientific field seeks to shed light on the causes of behavioral and psychological outcomes in an effort to develop intellectual frameworks (or *theories* or *paradigms*) that can help guide future research in this area, with an eye toward increasing our understanding of behavior and psychological processes.

As is true of any scientific area, psychology has both basic and applied elements. Work that is *basic* is focused on advancing knowledge. For instance, my research team at SUNY New Paltz recently published a paper that examines the personality correlates of relative Neanderthal overlap (see Geher et al., 2017). (Importantly, in this study, we mean *Neanderthal* in the literal sense, pertaining to the ancient species of hominids that roamed the earth alongside our own *Homo sapien* ancestors. I am not referring to any derogatory meanings of the word.) In short, we studied people who had had their genomes mapped. Personal genomic companies like 23andMe provide information on how much Neanderthal overlap one's genome has (this percentage varies from about 0% to 4%). We then gave out personality scales to these same individuals. Using various statistical procedures, we came to find that people who scored higher in Neanderthal overlap were more likely than others to show autistic tendencies and to report having lower levels of social support in their lives. Why did we do this research? Honestly, because we were curious! Upon learning about this idea of Neanderthal overlap based on personal genomic technology, we really wanted to see if relative Neanderthalness related in significant ways to psychological outcomes.

Now while we think that our research is super neat and sheds light on important questions regarding human origins and human behavior, we don't claim to have made any advances in terms of therapeutic techniques. We don't think that our findings will help reduce mental illness. We don't think that our findings will reduce anxiety and stress, at least not directly. This research is a classic instance of basic research—we did the research because we had questions related to psychology that we were curious about—and, using our statistical and research methodological toolkit, we went ahead and addressed those questions. Along the way, we found out some interesting new things about the relationship between genetic Neanderthal overlap and modern human psychological functioning. So when some people (such as researchers like myself) refer to themselves as *psychologists*, they often mean that they are basic psychologists who focus on research. Sometimes these folks will use the term *behavioral scientist*, which, I think, captures this field well.

On the other hand, we have fields of *applied* psychology. Some people who work in the field of psychology don't do any research at all. And that's OK! In fact, there are many areas of applied psychology out there. Some people are professional *therapists* or *counselors*. This is sort of the prototype of what people think of when they think of the term *psychologist*. Psychologists of this kind see clients who have various mental health issues and try to help these people using a variety of techniques (which might include cognitive behavior therapy, Skinnerian applied behavioral analysis, psychopharmacological therapies, etc.). In fact, there are many kinds of counselors or therapists, including the following:

- mental health counselors (master's or doctoral level),
- school counselors (master's or doctoral level),
- licensed clinical social worker (master's or doctoral level),
- clinical psychologists (doctoral level), and
- counseling psychologists (master's or doctoral level).

Further, many applied psychologists work outside the field of mental health, using their psychological education to help with various other kinds of issues, such as education, business, or health. With this in mind, note that some people who are *psychologists* work in applied fields such as

- industrial–organizational psychology (psychology applied to the business world; master's or doctoral level),
- health psychology (psychology applied in health contexts such as hospitals; master's or doctoral level),
- educational psychology (psychology applied in educational settings; master's or doctoral level),
- school psychology (psychology applied specifically to help students in need within the schools; master's or doctoral level), and
- quantitative psychology (psychology that uses statistics and mathematical modeling to address a broad array of issues; master's or doctoral level).

In a sense, applied psychologists are to basic psychologists as engineers are to physicists. Basic psychologists do work on helping us understand the nature of human behavior, and applied psychologists use findings from basic psychologists to make a difference. Similarly, basic physicists conduct work to help us best understand the physical world, while engineers use findings and principles of physics to do things like build bridges or airplanes. Neither is "better" than the other; both areas of work are essential for helping us to (a) best understand what it means to be human and (b) improve the human condition.

Just to make things slightly more complex, note that much work is done in what we might called *applied psychological research*. This is actually scientific research designed to address specific applied kinds of questions. For instance, a therapist who uses a mixture of psychodynamic and behavioral therapies might conduct a study to see which form of therapy is more effective in reducing anxiety in his or her clients. Or an educational psychologist might conduct a study to see if learning based on group projects is superior to learning based on lectures. Here, we have research being done, but it is being done for a very specific applied purpose (unlike basic research, which is conducted primarily to advance knowledge in a broader sense).

# The American Psychological Association's Five Goals for the Psychology Major

The American Psychological Association (APA) is the largest professional organization representing psychology in the United States, with more than 100,000 members. APA started in 1892 with G. Stanley Hall of Clark University as its first president. Since that time, APA has become a dominant force in advancing the field of psychology, having a major annual convention as well as a publishing arm that produces many high-caliber, peer-reviewed journals and books in the field. APA takes its role in advancing the field seriously and produces guidelines on various aspects of work in the field (such as the renowned *Publication Manual of the American Psychological Association* [APA, 2010] and *Graduate Study in Psychology* [APA, 2019]). In the past few decades, APA has taken to providing guidelines to help standardize and shape undergraduate curricula in psychology programs. This is a fancy way of saying that APA provides guidance on what all psychology majors should be learning.

Based on extensive research and deliberation, APA's (2013) *APA Guidelines for the Undergraduate Psychology Major* are not only well thought out, but they have also shaped the educational experiences of thousands of students to develop the kind of understanding of the field that is necessary to succeed after graduation. I know that I can recount dozens, if not hundreds, of success stories of students who have graduated from my own program, which strongly matches the APA criteria.

So, what are the APA goals for undergraduate psychology major programs?

I present them briefly here and elaborate on them in the remainder of the chapter.

- *Goal 1: Knowledge Base:* Understanding key content related to behavior and psychological processes
- *Goal 2: Scientific Inquiry and Critical Thinking:* Developing the intellectual skills needed to conduct and critically examine psychological research
- *Goal 3: Ethical and Social Responsibility in a Diverse World:* Understanding and appreciating diversity among people and developing an approach to the world that helps advance the greater good
- *Goal 4*: *Communication:* Presenting ideas and research regarding psychology effectively, in both written and oral formats
- *Goal 5: Professional Development:* Acquiring experiences within the curriculum, such as joining a faculty research team or doing an internship for credit, to gain the kinds of hands-on experiences need to succeed in the future

## Goal 1: Knowledge Base

When I was 18 years old, I had no clue how big a field psychology is. Given that it deals with behavior and psychological processes across any animal species, you can see that it is an enormous area of inquiry. The APA's *knowledge base* goal for psychology majors focuses on this fact. Psychology can be broken into many subareas. Some college programs divide the field into clusters such as the following:

- developmental psychology (how psychological processes change across the life span);
- social and personality psychology (dealing with how situations and individual dispositions shape behavior);
- abnormal, clinical, and counseling psychology (with a focus on psychopathology);
- behavioral and cognitive neuroscience (focusing on the physiological factors that underlie behavior and thought);
- cognition, language, and learning (addressing basic cognitive and learning processes that underlie behavior);

- applied psychology (including such areas as industrial/organizational psychology, sports psychology, and educational psychology); and/or
- theoretical perspectives (focusing on the history of the field along with particular frameworks or theories designed to help us advance the field of psychology).

These clusters are samples; APA does not dictate which particular clusters a department uses to organize the knowledge base of the major. What is important here is this: Psychology professors need to make sure that all students who graduate with the psychology major take classes that represent all of these different areas of knowledge. Therefore, it is typical for colleges to use a menu format to describe the degree track course requirements. For instance, there might be a developmental psychology category, and students can pick one of three classes that all deal with the theme of development.

This is all important so that you can see why you need to take classes from certain clusters. For instance, a psychology department might have a cluster called *Physiology, Learning, and Cognition*. The classes in this category can be more challenging than the classes in other categories—and you might find yourself struggling through one of your assignments, say, in Physiological Psychology, wondering why you have to take it. Well the answer is simple: This category represents a major area of psychology, and no one who graduates with a major in psychology should have little to no understanding of this particular part of the world of psychology. APA's knowledge-base goal is based on the idea that all areas of psychology are important and that any student majoring in psychology should be exposed to each of the basic areas.

# Goal 2: Scientific Inquiry and Critical Thinking

As you will see, the field of psychology is much more about scientific research than most people realize off the bat. Psychologists use a variety of statistical and methodological approaches to asking and answering questions related to behavior. As such, it is important that students who graduate with degrees in psychology develop these skills as part of their education.

The standard way for the APA's *Scientific Inquiry and Critical Thinking* goal to be reached is through rigorous required coursework in statistics and psychological research methods. Through these classes, students gain important skills, which usually include a combination of training in statistical calculations by hand, along with training in advanced statistical software such as the Statistical Package for Social Sciences or R. With this training, you'll be able to conduct your own research. And you will be able to critically examine research conducted by others. A graduate with a psychology degree should never hear a finding about human behavior and just accept it! These courses in your psychology curriculum provide you the tools that you will need to critically evaluate research conducted in the field.

# Goal 3: Ethical and Social Responsibility in a Diverse World

At the end of the day, a college education is all about training the leaders of the future. In the field of psychology, we take this very seriously. APA's goal related to ethical and social responsibility, with a focus on diversity, emphasizes this point. Ethical issues emerge in many facets of the work of professional psychologists. Researchers run into ethical quandaries regularly, wondering if they should deceive participants about the goal of a study, wondering if some particular experimental manipulation that causes stress is appropriate, and so on. And applied psychologists, such as psychotherapists, also regularly run into ethical issues. If someone in therapy reveals a suicidal thought, for instance, what should a therapist do? In classes such as psychological research methods and counseling techniques, students learn about these ethical issues along with best practices in dealing with them.

An important element of this goal deals with diversity, which is often embedded into psychology curricula. Human beings come in all shapes and sizes, varying from one another in such facets as gender, age, cultural background, and so forth. Diversity is an important issue across the psychology curriculum and several classes that you will take along the way, such as social psychology, deal directly with issues of diversity.

# Goal 4: Communication

I always tell my students that knowing something doesn't matter at all if you are not able to express that knowledge to others. Knowledge ultimately only matters in a social context. That is why you'll be doing some writing as part of your coursework in psychology. Writing in psychology is, in fact, quite different from writing in other fields, and it takes a great deal of direct mentorship to develop the needed skills to do this effectively. Your psychology curriculum will likely have at least one (gulp!) writing-intensive class in which students write multiple drafts of APA-formatted papers that undergo deep scrutiny from the instructor. This scrutiny, by the way, is not "being mean!" The more ink a professor puts on a paper, the more he or she is putting time into helping the student develop this important skill. The more students write and receive feedback, the better!

In addition to communicating in writing, aspiring psychologists should get used to giving oral presentations on psychological topics. Being able to express one's ideas in an oral presentation format is, simply, a useful life skill—and the more you practice it, the better. Many classes in the psychology curriculum have required oral presentations. While you're sweating through your next speech, it might help to think of the experience as your instructor's gift to the future you!

# Goal 5: Professional Development

You're in college partly so you can get a great job and partly so you can make a positive mark on the world. APA's professional-development goal is all about that. In many psychology majors, there are elements of the curriculum that provide students with professional-development opportunities. These may include one or more classes that comprise an internship. In an internship class, students will usually meet once a week with other students in a class with a professor who is expert in applied psychology, and then each student would also spend a certain number of hours at a *site* (such as working with a local psychotherapist) under the direct supervision of an expert practitioner. Often, a psychology program might have multiple classes that include internship-like experiences. Further, it is often the case that a student can do multiple internships for credit during his or her time in the program.

Many undergraduate psychology programs also have solid research opportunities for students. Often, this will include a class called *independent study* or something similar, which is a catchall course used for students to do any number of educational experiences for credit. These experiences are often truly invaluable as they really give students the kinds of hands-on experiences that map onto the real world. If these opportunities aren't spelled out in the requirements for your major or in any of your syllabi, I recommend seeking them out yourself (more details on how to do this in Chapter 8).

# The Bottom Line

APA's goals for undergraduate psychology curricula are designed to make sure that students receive a broad education in the field while also developing important analytical and presentational skills along the way, not to mention a sense of ethics and social responsibility, which I'll discuss in Chapter 2. When I started in a psychology program years ago, I didn't understand why some classes were required. I also didn't understand what psychology even was, now that I look back at it! So I understand if this is your starting point too.

I'm of the opinion that a rigorous psychology program that requires students to take coursework from across the entire discipline of psychology is essential for producing the next generation of leaders in the field of psychology. In addition, I endorse all five of the goals laid out in the *APA Guidelines for the Undergraduate Psychology Major*. You can find the full text of the *Guidelines* online; for quick reference, I've summarized the goals for you in an infographic (see Figure 1.1).

FIGURE 1.1

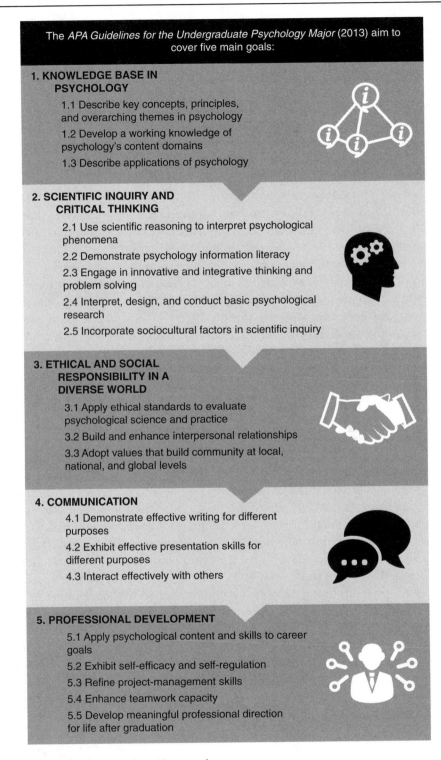

The *APA Guidelines for the Undergraduate Psychology Major* (2013) aim to cover five main goals:

**1. KNOWLEDGE BASE IN PSYCHOLOGY**

1.1 Describe key concepts, principles, and overarching themes in psychology

1.2 Develop a working knowledge of psychology's content domains

1.3 Describe applications of psychology

**2. SCIENTIFIC INQUIRY AND CRITICAL THINKING**

2.1 Use scientific reasoning to interpret psychological phenomena

2.2 Demonstrate psychology information literacy

2.3 Engage in innovative and integrative thinking and problem solving

2.4 Interpret, design, and conduct basic psychological research

2.5 Incorporate sociocultural factors in scientific inquiry

**3. ETHICAL AND SOCIAL RESPONSIBILITY IN A DIVERSE WORLD**

3.1 Apply ethical standards to evaluate psychological science and practice

3.2 Build and enhance interpersonal relationships

3.3 Adopt values that build community at local, national, and global levels

**4. COMMUNICATION**

4.1 Demonstrate effective writing for different purposes

4.2 Exhibit effective presentation skills for different purposes

4.3 Interact effectively with others

**5. PROFESSIONAL DEVELOPMENT**

5.1 Apply psychological content and skills to career goals

5.2 Exhibit self-efficacy and self-regulation

5.3 Refine project-management skills

5.4 Enhance teamwork capacity

5.5 Develop meaningful professional direction for life after graduation

The psychology major: Five goals.

# Making a Difference

## How the Psychology Curriculum Cultivates Ethical and Socially Responsible Leadership

2

A s a student, you are often focused on the details of your studies. *What is going to be on the exam? How is this professor going to grade the paper? Do I really have to read all of those chapters?!* . . .

Sometimes it's good to step back and think about the broader goals of what you are doing. *What is the point of all of these classes? What are these professors trying to achieve?*

The American Psychological Association's (APA's; 2013) *APA Guidelines for the Undergraduate Psychology Major* Goal 3, Ethical and Social Responsibility in a Diverse World, helps to provide a big-picture framework for understanding the point of all of the work that you are doing in your psychology classes. That's why I decided to present this goal first in the book, even though it's number 3 in the *Guidelines* document. As psychology professors see it, they are building the future leaders of the world, providing them with not only important knowledge and skills but also important insights into issues surrounding equity and social responsibility. Professors want the young people who graduate from their programs to be smart and knowledgeable, but they also want students to have a sense of social responsibility. The world is unstable, and to be fully forthright, the future is pretty uncertain right now. Ethically and socially responsible leaders who see themselves as true citizens of the world are needed to help get this world back on track. APA suggests that psychology programs be designed to underscore these points.

http://dx.doi.org/10.1037/0000127-002
*Own Your Psychology Major! A Guide to Student Success*, by G. Geher

# What Does It Mean to Be an Ethical and Socially Responsible Student?

This chapter elaborates on APA's goal regarding ethical and social responsibility. This broad goal of the major breaks into three specific learning outcomes. When you finish your psychology major, you should be able to do the following:

3.1 Apply ethical standards to evaluate psychological science and practice
3.2 Build and enhance interpersonal relationships
3.3 Adopt values that build community at local, national, and global levels

So let's think a bit about how your work in the major, and your work during your college years more broadly, will help develop these attributes in yourself. And let's think about what they mean in practical terms.

# Apply Ethical Standards to Evaluate Psychological Science and Practice

Outcome 3.1 of the *APA Guidelines* focuses on applying ethical standards to psychological science and practice. You will have opportunities during your time in the major to learn about these ethical standards as well as to demonstrate an understanding of these standards in your own work.

We've already discussed how the field of psychology has a *bifurcate* (i.e., two-sided) nature, in terms of having distinct basic and applied components. So it is important to consider ethical standards as they bear on both research and applications/practice.

Psychological researchers deal with ethical issues regularly. In designing research, we need to consider how to avoid issues such as the ones addressed in the following questions:

- Will participants in our research be deceived?
- Will participants in our research possibly be in physical pain?
- Will participants in our research experience psychological pain?
- Will participants in our research possibly have long-term psychological effects as a result of being in our research?
- Will participants in our research provide any personal information that could, if known, hurt their reputations?
- Will the participants formally have the opportunity to consent to be in the study before data collection begins?
- Will it be made clear to participants that they will be able to terminate their participation in the study at any time for any reason without a penalty to themselves?
- Will the data be stored in a de-identified manner (i.e., so that the participants' names are not connected with their responses)?
- Will participants be provided the opportunity to learn about the point of the study after data collection is completed?

When we are collecting psychological data from other people, we really have to take factors such as these into account. Remember, our point in collecting data in a psychological study is to find out something about human nature in a general sense; it is decidedly *not* to mess with the people who are in our actual study!

To explore this topic in more detail, consider one of the most famous studies in psychology, known as the Stanford Prison Experiment, in which college students were randomly assigned to take on the role of either prisoner or guard in the basement of an academic building over several days. The researchers (Haney, Banks, & Zimbardo, 1973) were interested in understanding the impact of social roles on behavior, asking questions such as whether becoming sadistic was an inherent feature of being in a role of prison guard. Famously, after a few days, the experiment had to be called off. It got out of hand! Some students who were in the guard role were incredibly sadistic. Some students in the prisoner role found themselves to be enormously stressed by the experience. In short, the researchers really messed with these people (albeit unintentionally). This study, and others from that same time period, led to large-scale conversations about ethics in psychological research. Today, we have national-level guidelines regarding ethics in research on human subjects as a result, including the APA (2017) *Ethical Principles of Psychologists and Code of Conduct*.

In classes such as Psychological Research Methods, you will learn the ins and outs of ethical issues that surround research in psychology. You will also learn about the oversight processes for data collection with human subjects, including learning about special groups that exist on college campuses, usually called the institutional review board (IRB), the human research ethics board (HREB), or something similar. These boards are essentially required for any institution where human research takes place. In fact, research institutions that do not have a formal board of this kind are ineligible for federal monies from the government—so it's pretty much the law!

The IRB (or comparable board) typically comprises faculty from the university, along with at least one member of the broader community. Using a variety of formal protocols, forms, and procedures, they take steps to make sure that proposed research meets all relevant ethical standards before being conducted. As a psychology major, you will learn about this process, and you will likely even complete the relevant IRB paperwork at some point (probably in your Psychological Research Methods class) to help advance your understanding of these issues. These experiences will help you learn the details of ethics in human subject research. Honestly, this stuff may feel a bit like going to the dentist, but it truly is a critical part of your psychology education.

Outcome 3.1 of the *APA Guidelines* also focuses on ethical standards in psychological practice. Here, we are talking more about work in the applied areas, such as in counseling or in industrial/organizational psychology. During your undergrad years, you will likely take part in one of various internship opportunities, such as working under the tutelage of an expert applied psychologist or counselor in your area.

Given that students in these kinds of applied positions are dealing with actual people in a counseling-related capacity, issues of ethical and social responsibility are absolutely critical. Mental health issues in industrialized societies and on college campuses are at an all-time high (see Srivastava, 2009). Levels of depression and anxiety seem to be particularly on the increase, with more students seeking counseling for these kinds of issues than has ever been the case in the past. Students who are working with others who are experiencing such emotional turmoil, even in an internship capacity, have a great deal of responsibility on their hands. Ethical issues in this kind of work address questions such as the following:

- Is a client a potential harm to him- or herself?
- Is a client a potential harm to others?
- Should a client be recommended for hospitalization?
- Should local law enforcement be brought in regarding a client's situation?
- Should the university administration be made aware of mental health issues surrounding a particular individual?
- Is the privacy of the individual being sufficiently protected?
- Is a client made fully aware of all of his or her rights?
- Is each client being addressed respectfully and empathically?
- Are techniques being used to improve the condition of a client based on empirical findings that demonstrate that they are effective techniques?
- Is the cultural background of the individual being effectively taken into account?
- Is the gender identity of the individual being effectively taken into account?

In various courses in the psychology curriculum, issues related to ethics and social responsibility in applied work in psychology are presented. You would learn about such issues in classes related to abnormal psychology, counseling psychology, and clinical psychology, for instance. Ideally, you would make it a point to do an internship during your undergraduate experience. Along the way, you would typically have two supervisors: (a) the official instructor of the internship class and (b) the site supervisor. Both of these individuals will help model appropriate behavior in dealing with clients and others relevant to the experience. The hands-on experiences that you will obtain if you choose to do an internship will likely provide you invaluable educational opportunities related to ethics and social responsibility in the realm of applied psychology.

# Build and Enhance Interpersonal Relationships

Outcome 3.2 is all about building and enhancing interpersonal relationships. No matter where you end up after college, you'll be working with people—that's a given, even if your job is focused more on manufacturing or design rather than human services. Your experience in the psychology major should prepare you for working effectively with others by a variety of means. Given the content of psychology, several classes in the curriculum will help elucidate issues related to interpersonal relationships. Coursework in social psychology, for instance, regularly includes content on the factors that underlie interactions in interpersonal relationships. Courses in counseling, personality psychology, and developmental psychology similarly will provide much *didactic* (textbook-based) information on the nature of interpersonal relationships.

In the psychology major, you will also have many opportunities to build and enhance all kinds of constructive interpersonal relationships related to the curricular experience. You will work with faculty members (professors) who will help guide your journey. Your work with faculty members will take place in many contexts, including (a) in the classroom, (b) during office hours, (c) as part of group projects (such as being on a research team with a professor), and (d) at events of your academic community (such as end-of-semester events). All things considered, the more that you interact and work directly with faculty members, the richer your experience in the major should be. Students who get to know the faculty members in a department well have a leg up in terms of all kinds of opportunities, including opportunities for research collaboration, traveling to conferences, internships, leadership in student organizations, and participation in extracurricular events, for example. Developing solid working relationships with faculty members is one of the top ways that a student can make sure that he or she is on the fast path to success.

In addition to developing interpersonal skills by working directly with faculty members, you will have opportunities to work directly with other students. This will come in the form of group projects for classes, collaborations in student clubs and organizations, collaborative projects on research teams, and more. The hands-on experiences that you receive in working with other psychology students during your academic journey will lead to some of the most important learning outcomes that you will find along the way. If you find it hard to get along with others or if you are kind of shy, then I say this: See your college years as something of a reset. You can really go full throttle into the community and work closely with others even if this has not been your style in the past. College is famous for its ability to provide these opportunities.

Here are some specific ways to build a strong social identity within the context of being a psychology major:

- Join study groups for your psychology classes.
- Join a psychology club and attend/organize regular meetings.
- Join clubs and organizations related to interests of yours that are outside of psychology (even if these are interests that are brand-new to you).
- Attend social events that are organized by the Psychology Department (such as end-of-year get-togethers).
- Participate in panels on such topics as graduate school or psychology careers.

In any case, whether you find yourself in a research laboratory or working in a county agency that supports people with various mental illnesses—or anything in between—you are going to be working with people. As such, I suggest that you take advantage of as many opportunities as possible during your undergraduate years to advance your skills and experiences in this area.

# Adopt Values That Build Community at Local, National, and Global Levels

Outcome 3.3 focuses on adopting values that build community at local, national, and global levels. As I've written about extensively (see Geher, 2014), humans are a communal ape. In fact, evolutionary scientists who have examined human uniqueness have made a strong case that our tendency to form communities, often across lines of kinship (i.e., outside of our own families), is one of the core features of what it means to be human (see Bingham & Souza, 2009; Wilson, 2007).

As Outcome 3.3 of the *APA Guidelines* suggests, communities exist at a multitude of levels. Take me, for instance. I live in a small neighborhood—there are about 15 houses on our street. All the neighbors know each other; we look out for each other. We regularly have block parties, and we see ourselves as a community. I'm also a member of the psychology department at my institution, which is another community entirely—one consisting of other faculty members, staff members, students, and alumni. We see ourselves as a community, working toward common goals (such as cultivating student success).

But that's not all. As an academic who studies evolutionary psychology, I find myself in the broader evolutionary psychology, which is truly international. I publish in international journals on this topic, I sit on the editorial boards of multiple journals related to this topic, I post on Facebook groups related to this topic, and I even started an intellectual society on this topic. The international evolutionary psychology community is, in fact, a community. And there are several regional, statewide, and national communities that I identify with as well.

As a psychology student, you will be exposed to communities of various types. Where you live is a community, whether it's in a residence hall, a shared apartment, or with your own family. Each of these communities can be built up or broken down, depending on the ethical choices its individual members make. Depending on your living situation, you may have some new choices opening up for you in your residential community, such as

- when to say yes or no to a party invite and whether to use alcohol or drugs;
- how to speak up for yourself in your personal relationships, such as when your roommate fails to respect your property or when you don't consent to something a romantic partner wants to do; and
- what details about your personal life you should disclose to others, such as your schedule of coming and going or how much money you are making if you have a part-time job.

Each class you take is also, in effect, a community. The group of students and faculty members in your department form a community. Each student club that you join is also a community unto itself. All of these experiences should help you develop skills related to effectively working in a communal context—a group of people with unique interests all working together toward a common goal. For my money, at the end of the day, people who contribute most effectively to communities are the richest among us.

# Going Above and Beyond as a Psychology Student

Ethical and social responsibility is a value you can practice from your very first day as a student. In case you haven't noticed, the world is a little messy right now. And it is up to all of us to get this world back on track. This is partly why your psychology professors care so much about you understanding the value of community and the details regarding how to best build well-functioning communities across multiple levels. My hope is that when you graduate as a psychology major, you will see yourself as a global citizen, with a responsibility to help leave this world a better place at the end of the day.

Much of life is what you make it—the result of your choices. It's easy to make choices that help you follow the path of least resistance. Such a "meeting minimal standards" approach to life works just fine. But we've really only got one chance in life, and while meeting minimal standards may be alright, consistently going above and beyond has the capacity to set one onto a path of greatness. Further, going above and beyond has the capacity to set one apart as a true leader in his or her community. Working to help advance the goals of the broader community is exactly the kind of thing that sets students apart. And I believe that is the kind of mind-set that the world needs right now.

With all this in mind, here are some specific examples of how a psychology student can go above and beyond and help cultivate an identity as a global citizen:

- volunteering with at least one organization (at most universities, there are dozens available at any given time);
- joining at least one club (there are tons of them) and working to take on a leadership position at some point with a club (secretary, treasurer, vice president, president, communications officer, etc.);
- taking at least one internship class (these days, nearly all majors offer internship opportunities within the major itself);
- joining a professor in a collaborative research effort—all professors are engaged in some level of scholarly work and could usually benefit from having students collaborating with them. Such work often can be done for college credit and can lead to great outcomes, such as presentations at conferences or publications;
- being that student who attends every class, does all the work to the best of his or her ability, and never asks to take a makeup exam. There is a special place for such students. And students who demonstrate this kind of dependability are well positioned to help be community leaders into the future.

# Jaime's Story: An Example of a Student Who Cared

The State University of New York (SUNY) New Paltz, where I work, has a long-standing Undergraduate Psychology Association (UPA). This student club includes between about 15 and 40 volunteer members at any given time, who are always under stellar leadership. The club takes its charge seriously. The members organize regular meetings during which they discuss possible initiatives. They invite professors and therapists to talk about their work with the group. They help co-organize our departmental end-of-year trivia party and our annual departmental award ceremony and barbecue. They help the department organize the major events that we hold with regularity. In short, the UPA has a legacy of greatness, and at any given time, the current students in the group seem to embrace this ethos.

Years ago, there was a young first-year student named Jaime—a bright, quiet kid from Long Island. She was interested in studying psychology and started talking with several of her professors—talking about the content of our classes but also talking about what kinds of opportunities might be available for her to do something great. Several of us encouraged her to join the UPA, which at that point was not very well attended. She joined and quickly found herself with an officer position.

Within a year or two, she was suddenly the president of the UPA, which now had dozens of students regularly attending their meetings and events. And they put on awesome, creative events, such as Psychology Jeopardy (which often found students beating out faculty, somewhat embarrassingly). They worked closely with faculty to help us provide above-and-beyond experiences to all students in the community. Under Jaime, the UPA was a force! She then went on to receive a doctorate and is now teaching courses related to cognitive neuroscience at the college level.

The UPA has since stayed on this trajectory. Under Jaime's leadership, certain norms were put into place—for example, the group came to regularly organize events and activities for the entire community, making sure that their work had benefits beyond themselves. The UPA has all the hallmarks of a civic-minded, community-focused organization. Leader after leader of that group has continued the momentum, with the UPA consistently being one of the most active student organizations on campus. And I have full faith that the active members of this group will see all kinds of success in their futures as a result.

So, why should you go above and beyond as a student? Why should you choose to take on leadership roles? Why should you prioritize community ahead of self? Students have lots of choices to make. Sure, you can choose to do the minimum. You can choose to go to most of your classes, come home, and sit around playing video games. Or you can choose to look for opportunities to go above and beyond and make a positive difference for others. In my experience, the students who choose to make a positive difference not only accomplish great things, but they also, often unwittingly, pave roads of success for their own futures. And they are the ones among us who will lead our communities forward.

# The Bottom Line

You're in college not just to increase your knowledge and skills so you can get a great job, but also to grow as a human being. The *APA Guidelines* regarding ethical and social responsibility clearly reflect this fact. Ethical considerations are relevant to research, as well as to all kinds of practices related to the psychological professions, and yes, even to your daily life. Anything you can do to advance your ability to work with others from a diverse array of backgrounds is good, because humans are a communal ape and working with others toward common, communal goals is what we do when we are at our best.

# KNOWLEDGE BASE: THE CONTENT OF PSYCHOLOGY

# II

We have already discussed the two large areas of *basic* and *applied* psychology. However, within each of these larger categories are many specific content areas that comprise the meat and potatoes of the field. The next few chapters will, I hope, give you a sense of the broad array of areas that comprise our field. Chapter 3 explicitly addresses Goal 1 of the American Psychological Association's (APA's; 2013) *APA Guidelines for the Undergraduate Psychology Major*: Knowledge Base in Psychology. Chapters 4 and 5 offer several examples to illustrate what I feel are the two most important concepts that cut across the knowledge base of psychology and that I believe will endure even as the field matures and expands.

## Chapter 3: The Broad Nature of Psychology Content: How Do These Different Topics Relate to Each Other?

Psychology is an extremely broad field. Anything related to behavior and/or mental processes fits within the broader category of "psychology." Thus, one psychologist might study how rats learn to avoid painful shocks, whereas another might focus his or her work on understanding predictors of self-esteem in elderly populations. And these examples represent mere slices of the enormous field of psychology. This chapter introduces the foundational ideas of psychology (including basic and applied psychology) along with brief summaries of the various core areas of psychology. Along the way, the importance of each of these different areas is described—coupled with ideas on how the many seemingly disparate parts of psychology are interrelated.

# Chapter 4: Human Diversity and Human Universality: How We Are All the Same and How We Are All Unique

Most likely, your psychology major will include content on cross-cultural psychology (*how does behavior change as a function of cultural influences?*) as well as content related to the psychology of human universals (*why do people all across the globe show marked similarities in so many behavioral domains?*). Although the two concepts may seem to be at odds with each other, it is the very tension between them that keeps psychologists asking questions and expanding the field. Chapter 4 addresses the interplay between cultural causes of behavior and evolutionary causes of behavior.

# Chapter 5: Multifactorial Causation of Behavior: A Fact of Psychology

Chapter 5 expands on the idea of multiple causes of behavior presented in Chapter 4. Here, we directly address *multifactorial causation*. This concept is foundational to a strong understanding of psychology. The basic idea is that for any given behavior, causes exist at multiple levels concurrently (i.e., at the same time). So if someone has an unhealthy drug addiction, one psychologist might talk about the activation of the rewards center in the brain as the cause, another might talk about an unstable family situation as the cause, and yet another might point to peer pressure as the cause. In fact, it is quite possible that each of these factors may play a causal role in the outcome. Multifactorial causation provides us with a powerful and open-minded framework for understanding the entirety of human psychology.

# The Broad Nature of Psychology Content
## How Do These Different Topics Relate to Each Other?

3

The field of psychology is huge. This is one of the first lessons that you need to learn as a psychology major. People who identify as "psychologists" vary considerably from one another in terms of their area of research interest, the kind of data they collect, the theoretical perspectives used to drive their research, the phenomena they study, and more. And this all is in addition to the fact that some psychologists are purely applied practitioners and others are purely behavioral science researchers.

## Developing a Knowledge Base in Psychology

This chapter refers to Goal 1 from the *APA Guidelines for the Undergraduate Psychology Major* (American Psychological Association [APA], 2013): Knowledge Base in Psychology. This goal of the major breaks into three specific learning outcomes:

1.1 Describe key concepts, principles, and overarching themes in psychology
1.2 Develop a working knowledge of psychology's content domains
1.3 Describe applications of psychology

http://dx.doi.org/10.1037/0000127-003
*Own Your Psychology Major! A Guide to Student Success,* by G. Geher

The Knowledge Base goals essentially are designed to make sure that students are exposed to content that represents the different areas of psychology well. Let's start by examining the three learning outcomes of the Knowledge Base goals.

# Describe Key Concepts, Principles, and Overarching Themes in Psychology

While psychologists often don't see eye to eye with one another in terms of the best ways to approach psychological concepts, we usually at least agree that there is variety in terms of our field. Regardless of the content that one is studying within the field, there are definitely some key concepts that we all expect students to learn while under our watch. These can be broken into (a) theoretical perspectives, (b) key intellectual debates, (c) and statistical and methodological concepts. We make sure that the major introduces all students to these important intellectual concepts that underlie all the work in our field. Let's take a look at these ideas in turn and discuss how they are typically reflected in the major along the way.

## THEORETICAL PERSPECTIVES IN PSYCHOLOGY

Theoretical perspectives in the field can be thought of as frameworks used to ask and answer questions related to psychology. Some psychologists are hard-core *neuroscientists*, who think that we need to primarily understand what is going on in terms of the neurons in the brain to understand what human behavior is about. In contrast, *humanists* might see things entirely differently, studying all aspects of the psychological experience as they connect with meaning in one's life. Following is a brief summary of some of the basic theoretical perspectives that you should be exposed to during your time as a psychology student:

- *Behaviorism:* the idea that only observable behavior should be studied and that mental, nonobservable constructs, should be fully omitted from the field of psychology.
- *Neuroscience:* an area of inquiry that focuses on the physical substrates of behavior, based on the assumption that all behavior can be reduced to patterns of neural activity.
- *Evolutionary psychology:* a perspective that focuses on Darwin's ideas related to evolution and that assumes that all behavior is the product of evolutionary forces and should be studied as such.
- *Social constructionism:* similar to what some call *postmodernism*, an approach that assumes that all psychological reality is the product of social constructions—things that people "create" in social interactions.
- *Psychodynamics:* based on the work of Freud, an approach that sees human behavior as largely the results of unconscious activity, often connected with unfulfilled sexual urges and desires.

- *Humanism:* an approach that sees all people as inherently good and that focuses on ways that we can get people to reach their level of optimal functioning.
- *Positive psychology:* an approach that focuses on the positive aspects of the psychological experience, studying such concepts as happiness, gratitude, and the creation of well-functioning human communities.
- *The cognitive perspective:* an approach to psychology that focuses on information processing, viewing the human mind as analogous to a computational machine and psychological processes as a series of computations.

As with anything in psychology, given its broad nature, this list is likely incomplete. But it provides a good survey of some of the basic theoretical perspectives that you will learn about in the major—frameworks that drive the research in the field. As a student, it's often useful to think about whether research being done relates directly (or indirectly) to one or more of these perspectives.

Also, you can now see why APA wants to make sure that diversity in theoretical perspectives is included in the major. Imagine a program that only had neuroscientists, for instance, on the faculty. Students in that program would get a rigorous education in the physiological underpinnings of psychology, to be sure—but they would not have a great sense of the many other basic approaches to understanding and studying human psychology. As such, students from such a narrow program would miss out on opportunities to be trained for many of the careers outside of neuroscience.

## KEY INTELLECTUAL DEBATES

Just as there are various basic theoretical perspectives that underlie how psychologists do their work, there are also some very central intellectual debates that drive the work of psychologists. These debates often pit two strong ideas regarding some issue against one another. As I usually tell my students, the "right answer" is usually somewhere in the middle! This said, there are definitely major debates in the field that have a large influence on how work in the field progresses. Some of the more conspicuous such debates are as follows:

- *Nature Versus Nurture.* This debate focuses largely on whether inherent, biological factors or developmental, "experiential" factors play the dominant role in shaping who people are and how they behave. Think about your own level of extraversion, or how outgoing you are. Someone who appeals to the "nature" side of this debate might argue that there are genes that play a large role in determining levels of extraversion and that you were "born" to have a certain level of extraversion. Someone on the "nurture" side might, rather, point toward research on how important one's environmental upbringing is in shaping levels of extraversion as well as a suite of other basic personality traits.
- *Materialism Versus Constructionism.* Some academic psychologists focus on the physical (i.e., material) underpinnings of behavior, based on the idea that at the end of the day, behavior is nothing more than the result of neural activity. Constructionists, on the other hand, downplay material causes of behavior and

instead focus on how psychological reality is ultimately found in the meaning that people give psychological concepts in social contexts. On this point, let's consider the psychological attribute of emotional responsivity, or the tendency to respond emotionally to various stimuli (Repacholi & Gopnik, 1997). A hardcore neuroscientist might see someone's high level of emotional responsivity as nothing more than a particular set of genes and a set of physiological structures, such as the reticular activation system, being calibrated a certain way. On the other hand, a constructionist might see someone who is seen as highly emotionally responsive as having been shaped to behave in an emotional manner based on various social roles and social expectations in one's community.

▪ *Person Versus Situation.* There is often debate regarding whether factors within people themselves cause their behaviors or if situational cues play a more critical role. *Dispositionists* focus on internal causes of behavior, such as personality traits or emotional states. *Situationists* focus more on factors in situations that exert influences on behavior. For instance, suppose that Joe is watching a Little League baseball game and just yelled out at the ump that he doesn't know what he's doing. A dispositionist might look to Joe's behavior and say that he has poor impulse control and an aggressive social style, while a situationist might ask more about the call that the ump made and about the behaviors of others in the crowd to examine how much the details of the situation may have affected Joe's actions.

▪ *Consistency Versus Change Across Development.* Whether people can change who they are across the life span is another hotly debated topic in psychology. Some argue that our personality becomes fixed during late childhood. Others argue that there is potential for change across the life span. Research into this issue is extremely intriguing, with some data suggesting that there is little change in one's basic character across life and other data suggesting just the opposite!

▪ *Cultural Universals Versus Cultural Variability.* Are people the same wherever you go? Some will say yes, and some will say no. To be sure, there are clearly ways that humans are the same across the globe. For instance, using a smile to express happiness seems to be a human universal. On the other hand, there seem to be important ways that one's culture shapes behavior. This is why religious activities often look quite different from one another across religious groups. The question of behavioral universality versus cultural variability is a hot one, and some of the best research being done by psychologists examines questions related to this particular debate.

## STATISTICAL AND METHODOLOGICAL CONCEPTS

A major part of the base knowledge that a student will obtain in a psychology major pertains to statistical and methodological concepts. Most undergraduate programs in psychology have courses in statistics and research methods. These classes, in fact, are so important in the major that they each get their own chapter later in this book! The idea here is that you need to understand basic statistical concepts, such as *hypothesis testing* and *effect size*, to be able to conduct your own research and to be able to critically examine research being presented by others. Further, you will need a broad array of research methodological tools in your intellectual toolbox to emerge as someone who has been well educated in the field of psychology. Methodological tools that you will acquire during your education will include an understanding of such concepts as the following:

- *internal validity*—the degree to which the outcome in an experiment can confidently be ascribed as being caused by an independent variable in the experiment;
- *external validity*—the degree to which the findings from the study are relevant to the real world;
- *randomization and experimental control*—the degree to which participants in different groups of an experiment were assigned by a random process, along with the degree to which the experimenter controls all possible confounding variables; and
- *construct validity*—the degree to which a measure in a study actually measures what it was designed to measure.

Chapters 6 and 7 provide basic introductions to these two general topics (statistics and research methods), so don't worry about the details of them quite yet. For now, just realize that part of the knowledge base that APA expects psychology students to acquire during their education includes foundations in statistics and research methods.

# Develop a Working Knowledge of Psychology's Content Domains

Most introductory psychology books are divided into basic areas (such as *Development*) that have several interrelated chapters included therein. Although the APA does not dictate which specific content areas are to be included, it is clear that it wants students to be required to learn some content in each of the basic areas of the field.

Chapter 1 included a sample list of content areas that represent the field well and might be included in a psychology major. These included (a) developmental psychology; (b) social and personality psychology; (c) abnormal, clinical, and counseling psychology; (d) behavioral and cognitive neuroscience; (e) cognition, language, and learning; (f) applied areas of psychology; and (g) theoretical perspectives.

The *APA Guidelines* include theoretical perspectives and applied areas as their own distinct elements of the major. Thus, the relevant meat-and-potatoes content areas from my list include the sections related to developmental, social/personality, abnormal/clinical, neuroscience, and language.

Importantly, there are multiple classes within any psychology program related to these various areas. For instance, a *developmental* area might have courses titled *Psychology of Infancy and Childhood*, *Psychology of Adolescence*, *Psychology of Adulthood*, and *Psychology of Aging*. The *social/personality* area might have courses titled *Social Psychology*,

*Social Perception, Personality Psychology, Emotion and Motivation,* and *Advanced Social Psychology.* And so forth.

Later in this chapter, you will find a full example of a Psychology Major Plan, including specific proposed classes for each of the content areas included in this section, to give you a sense of how these different conceptual areas might map onto a specific (if hypothetical) academic program in psychology. For now, it's important mostly to know that psychology has a broad array of topics and that the *APA Guidelines* place an emphasis on making sure that students have coursework that cuts across all of the basic areas of the field.

## Applications of Psychology

As described earlier, psychology, like any area of inquiry, can be broken into *basic* and *applied* sections. Often, when people think of applied psychology, they think of psychotherapy or mental health counseling. Although these are important areas of applied psychology, in fact, there are many more areas of applied psychology out there—and it's important that students of psychology are aware of this. Following is a list of areas that fall within the purview of applied psychology. As described in Chapter 1, in addition to the fields related to psychotherapy (such as clinical psychology), applied psychologists work in such field as industrial–organizational psychology (psychology in the workplace), educational psychology (psychology applied in educational settings), school and guidance counseling (psychology used to help guide and counsel middle and high school students), school psychology (psychology used to help assess students and provide performance programs), health psychology (psychology used in health settings such as hospitals), forensic psychology (psychology used to help solve crimes), clinical social work (helping people in difficult social and economic situations cope with stress and obtain needed resources), and sport and exercise psychology (psychology used to optimize fitness and sport outcomes). Some psychology curricula now also have a class titled Careers in Psychology, often a one-credit class that exposes students to several of the career paths that follow from a psychology major, which may include guest lectures from practitioners in the field.

Given the importance of preparing to meet the real world, it's essential that you obtain a strong understanding of the various applied areas that follow from a psychology major. As such, it's important that a psychology major plan includes opportunities to learn about these applied fields.

## A Sample Plan for a Psychology Major

To help you see how a specific psychology curriculum maps onto the APA goals, I present in Table 3.1 a hypothetical psychology plan. Note that this sample plan is exactly that: a sample. The psychology major at any particular school might differ in various ways from this sample plan, including number of credit hours required.

**TABLE 3.1**

**Sample Psychology Major Plan Based on American Psychological Association's (2013)**
*APA Guidelines for the Undergraduate Psychology Major*

| Category | Courses (credits) |
|---|---|
| Introduction (required) | ▪ Introductory Psychology I: Basic Scientific Approaches to Psychology (3)<br>▪ Introductory Psychology 2: Applied Approaches to Psychology (3)<br>▪ Careers in Psychology (1) |
| Scientific Inquiry (required) | ▪ Statistics for Psychology (4, including lab with SPSS software program)<br>▪ Research Methods for Psychology (4, including lab with SPSS and an intensive writing component and an oral presentation) |
| Capstone (required) | ▪ Advanced Seminar in Psychology (4, including an intensive writing component and an oral presentation) |
| Content Area 1: Theoretical Perspectives (Choose 1: 3 credits each) | ▪ History and Systems of Psychology (3)<br>▪ Positive Psychology (3)<br>▪ Cross-Cultural Psychology (3)<br>▪ Evolutionary Psychology (3) |
| Content Area 2: Applied Psychology (choose 1: 3 credits each) | ▪ Sport Psychology (3)<br>▪ Educational Psychology (3)<br>▪ Industrial/Organizational Psychology (3)<br>▪ Health Psychology (3) |
| Content Area 3: Development (choose 1: 3 credits each) | ▪ Psychology of Infancy and Childhood (3)<br>▪ Psychology of Adolescence (3)<br>▪ Psychology of Adulthood (3)<br>▪ Psychology of Aging (3) |
| Content Area 4: Mental Health (choose 1: 3 credits each) | ▪ Abnormal Psychology (3)<br>▪ Clinical and Counseling Psychology (3)<br>▪ Psychological Assessment (3)<br>▪ Stigma and Mental Illness (3) |
| Content Area 5: Neuroscience (choose 1: 3 credits each) | ▪ Cognitive Neuroscience (3)<br>▪ Behavioral Neuroscience (3)<br>▪ Animal Behavior (3)<br>▪ Hormones and Behavior (3) |
| Content Area 6: Cognition and Learning (choose 1: 3 credits each) | ▪ Psychology of Learning (3)<br>▪ Cognitive Psychology (3)<br>▪ Psychology of Language (3)<br>▪ Sensation and Perception (3) |
| Content Area 7: Social and Personality (choose 1: 3 credits each) | ▪ Social Psychology<br>▪ Personality Psychology<br>▪ Motivation and Emotion<br>▪ Psychology of Gender |
| Field Experience (choose 1: 3 credits each [except for the 0-credit-bearing Study Abroad Experience]) | ▪ Field Experience in Psychological Research (3)<br>▪ Internship in Psychology (3)<br>▪ Study Abroad |
| Experiential Component of Major | ▪ Experiential (0 credits; 12 half-hour units needed to complete major) |

*Note.* SPSS = Statistical Package for Social Sciences.

The "experiential" component is modeled after a requirement in the SUNY New Paltz psychology major. It includes 12 half-hour units of experiential work including such activities as acting as a participant in research, attending research talks or workshops by external scholars, and other extracurricular experiences that complement the content of the major.

Your school may encourage study abroad more strongly for language or business majors than for science and human services majors. I included it in the sample psychology major plan because, as I see it, studying abroad is considered a critical form of field experience, and all psychology majors are encouraged to partake.

To fulfill the sample plan depicted in Table 3.1, students must complete at least 49 total credits. Thus, students are encouraged to complete more than one class in each category if they are interested in doing so (two 3-credit classes must be taken beyond the minimal requirements). At your institution, there may also be "special topics" courses that you could, at the department faculty's discretion, count toward one of the categories required for your major.

## The Bottom Line

The field of psychology is extremely broad, including a wide range of topics related to behavior and psychological processes. The *APA Guidelines for the Undergraduate Psychology Major* take this breadth into account by recommending that students be exposed to the entire range of areas that comprise the field.

# Human Diversity and Human Universality

## How We Are All the Same and How We Are All Unique

4

As we saw in Chapter 3, the content of psychology is quite broad-reaching in scope. Chapters 4 and 5 continue to explore the knowledge base of psychology (Goal 1 from the *APA Guidelines for the Undergraduate Psychology Major*; American Psychological Association [APA], 2013), taking a deeper dive into two themes and critical debates that shape research in the field in important ways. The first such theme deals with culturally variable versus culturally universal psychological phenomena. In other words, just how universal are psychological phenomena across human groups? The second theme is about the many multilayered factors that cause human behaviors.

I'm devoting Chapters 4 and 5 to these themes because human diversity is integral to the *APA Guidelines*. In introducing the Five Goals, the *Guidelines* state that the learning outcomes within each goal should be "infused" with sociocultural conversations—these might include identity formation, power and access, privilege, and oppression. Although you and your professors may only chip away at huge societal challenges, like discrimination in our country or our world, you can be alert for opportunities to "[reap] the benefits of exploring differences in a meaningful way" (p. 39). Ideally, such opportunities will come up in more than one class or situation during your undergraduate years.

http://dx.doi.org/10.1037/0000127-004
*Own Your Psychology Major! A Guide to Student Success*, by G. Geher

This issue of universality versus cross-cultural variability plays out in a number of subareas in the field. Social psychologists who study the effects of culture on behavior are interested in whether social psychological phenomena, such as how humans choose long-term mating partners, varies importantly across human cultures. Developmental psychologists are often interested in the question of whether child-rearing varies across human groups and, if it does, how such variability affects development and behavior. Evolutionary psychologists are often interested in documenting human universality, trying to figure out whether certain psychological features play out the same across a broad range of human groups. And scholars who are interested in the psychology of gender often focus on the issue of whether gender roles are consistent or, instead, are variable across human cultural groups. The issue of culture's role on psychological processes cuts broadly and deeply across the various areas that serve as the foundation of the field of psychology.

# Diversity: A Curricular Goal as Well as a Fact of Life

One of the great advances in psychology over the past several decades has been the appreciation and integration of culture as a factor that is inextricably linked to psychological phenomena.

Human diversity comes in, well, a diversity of attributes! People vary from one another in terms of such *physical attributes* as

- height,
- weight,
- body shape,
- coloration,
- musculature

and more!

People vary from one another terms in *personality* in terms of

- extraversion,
- narcissistic tendencies,
- attachment style,
- open-mindedness,
- need for closure,
- creativity

and more!

People vary from one another in terms of *social attitudes* in terms of

- political orientation,
- religiosity,
- xenophobia

and more!

People vary from one another *culturally* in terms of

- a focus on individuals (*individualism*) versus collectives (*collectivism*),
- definition and role of family,
- treatment of the elderly,
- treatment of children,
- the emphasis on formal education

and more!

Cultures are diverse—we vary from one another dramatically along all kinds of dimensions, and this fact plays out in important ways when it comes to the nature of human psychology.

Of these different forms of diversity, cultural diversity has been a primary focus in the social sciences—and psychology is no exception. It turns out that cultural factors have broad-reaching effects across nearly all aspects of human psychological processes—even such basic processes as visual perception (see Nisbett, 2003).

To make things a bit more complex, it's interesting to note that while culture plays such a profound role in shaping psychological and behavioral processes, it's also the case that there are some profound cross-cultural universals in human psychology. One well-studied example is the tendency for people across any and all cultures to perceive a smile as a signal of happiness (see Ekman & Friesen, 1986).

This bifurcate reality of human psychology, focusing on the seemingly disparate facts of psychological cross-cultural variability and cross-cultural universality, is one of the most profound issues that underlies the entirety of modern work in the field of psychology. The remainder of this chapter explores these topics to help provide a new student in the field with intellectual tools needed to understand the various issues at hand.

# How Our Minds Make Cultural Shortcuts

Under ancestral conditions, when the human mind was taking form across eons of human evolutionary history, humans lived in small nomadic groups, capped at about 150 (see Dunbar, 1992). Under these conditions, people interacted generally with two kinds of others: kin and long-standing family connections. There were no strangers in one's clan. And the people you dealt with were pretty much the same people across your entire life span. On this basis, evolutionary psychologists like me conclude that human beings did not evolve to effectively deal with cultural diversity—and problems that we find in modern life that result from cross-cultural conflict (such as prejudice and religious persecution) are largely the result of this fact.

Many social psychological processes that have been uncovered help us understand the mechanics of cultural psychology, ultimately helping us understand why it is often so difficult to understand and appreciate the thoughts, attitudes, and beliefs of those who come from cultures that are different from our own. Following are summaries of some of the basic concepts in social psychology that underlie conflict when it comes to cross-cultural communications and interactions.

# Outgroup Homogeneity and the Stereotyping Mind

So here is a brief activity. I want you to conjure up two general groups of people:

- College students

and

- Truck drivers

Of these two groups, which do you think includes more within-group variability on physical, psychological, demographic, and cultural dimensions. In other words, in which group is there more variability among people within that group, (a) college students or (b) truck drivers?

I could be wrong, but my guess is that you might have chosen Option A: college students. And you probably have all kinds of reasons that you can provide for that. Colleges seek out diversity in applications. There are all kinds of colleges, which likely draw in all kinds of people as students. On the other side, you may note that truck drivers tend to be relatively homogenous in terms of gender and age (mostly middle-aged men), and you may further imagine truck drivers varying less from each other in terms of educational background (likely all having specialized training in truck driving) and perhaps even political attitudes.

I'm not saying whether you're right or wrong. You may know one or more truck drivers and have seen for yourself that they vary widely along many dimensions. What I am saying is this: People often demonstrate the *outgroup homogeneity bias* (see Haslam et al., 1996) when making judgments about people from another cultural background. That is, we tend to think that people in our own cultural group vary wildly from one another (*there are lots of different kinds of college students!*), whereas we tend to think that people from "different" cultural groups from our own tend to be very similar to one another (*oh, you know how all those truck drivers are!*).

In understanding the psychology of culture, it's important to understand how likely we are to demonstrate the outgroup homogeneity effect.

# Belief Perseverance

Stereotypes run deep, often to the point that we unconsciously hold stereotypes of others despite outwardly saying that we don't (see Greenwald, Schwartz, & Jordan, 1998). For a broad variety of reasons, stereotypes become entrenched in our psychology, and they often require active attention and effort on our part to get beyond them. One outcome of a mind that is prone toward stereotyping others is the phenomenon of *belief perseverance* (see Anderson, 1983). Human minds are funny things—they don't like to change! In fact, people often fail to change their opinions and attitudes in light of clear evidence suggesting that they are incorrect about something.

For an example of how resistant people are to changing their minds, consider the now-infamous 2016 presidential election in the United States. On the heels of that conspicuously divisive election, people who voted for Hillary Clinton were hard-pressed to allow any evidence to convince them that they voted for the wrong candidate. And those who voted for Donald Trump were similarly likely to stand by their guns, so to speak. Beliefs tend to persevere.

The entrenched nature of belief perseverance poses an important set of psychological problems when it comes to the psychology of culture. Not only do we, often against our own will, hold stereotypes of people from other cultures and see them as highly similar to one another, but for a host of social psychological reasons, we find it difficult to change our minds when it comes to these beliefs. Belief perseverance on top of stereotyping and on top of outgroup homogeneity makes for an ominous set of psychological barriers when it comes to interacting with people from cultures different from our own.

# Selective Exposure and Confirmation Bias

*Selective exposure* (see Hart et al., 2009), or the tendency to choose information that confirms our a priori (i.e., already existing) beliefs, really exacerbates the problems related to the psychology of culture. In a large-scale study examining the results of several existing studies on selective exposure (by the way, such a study of studies is called a *meta-analysis*), Hart and his colleagues (2009) found strong evidence that the selective exposure effect is a general effect. In other words, people do tend to seek out confirming rather than disconfirming information regularly, across a variety of contexts.

This selective exposure effect plays into a related phenomenon that we refer to as *confirmation bias* (see Nickerson, 1998), which is essentially the tendency to take actions that will ultimately confirm any preexisting biases that we may hold. So if Frank voted for Donald Trump, and Frank has the opportunity to read either an article titled "Trump's Tax Triumph" or one titled "Trump's Exploitation of the Working Class," Fred will likely choose the former, an article that is likely to confirm what Frank already believes. For a variety of reasons, we are uncomfortable with information that conflicts with our a priori view of the world (see Festinger & Carlsmith, 1959), and our choices in life often reflect this.

When it comes to dealing with people from other cultures, then, our tendency to take steps to confirm whatever we already believe provides a strong barrier to appreciating and understanding the actions, beliefs, and attitudes of people who come from cultures that are very different from our own.

# The False Consensus Effect

The tendency to focus our attention and energy on information that confirms our existing belief system has several effects on how we see the social world. One of the best-documented such effects is the *false consensus effect* (see Bauman & Geher, 2003). Put simply, the false consensus effect exists when people overestimate the degree to which others share their beliefs, traits, or characteristics. This effect can help explain the large-scale shock that many Democrats experienced after Donald Trump won the 2016 election (see Davis & Detrow, 2017). This election result was partly so surprising to so many people because dyed-in-the-wool Democrats had a hard time seeing "the other side." To many of them at that time, Donald Trump was simply not a viable candidate. Further, these people received all kinds of confirming information from others in their own particular social worlds. They were surrounded, in their own little cultural niches, by others who shared their views. And due to processes such as selective exposure, they were largely in the dark regarding perspectives other than their own. An outcome associated with this kind of reasoning would be false consensus—the belief that a higher proportion of others share their views than was actually the case. As we can see by the large-scale shock that followed the election among the nation's political left, it almost certainly was the case that Clinton supporters strongly and truly believed that a large majority of people in the nation (beyond the gap of 3 million people vis-à-vis the popular vote) agreed with their side.

# Failure to Allow for Variability in Construal

In a classic treatise on social psychological processes, Ross and Nisbett (1991) integrated information on a variety of concepts to arrive at this conclusion: When it comes to how we perceive others, we both (a) fail to appreciate the perspectives of others (especially when they differ from our own) and (b) fail to appreciate the fact that views among people in groups that we define as different from our own might vary considerably within that group. Thus, when it comes to cross-cultural communication and interaction, we often do not get how people in a different cultural group from our own see things, and, further, due to the outgroup homogeneity effect, we are not able to appreciate the fact that these others likely differ from one another in their views in important ways.

In combination, these social psychological biases and processes provide an important foundation regarding the need for cross-cultural psychology. Humans did not evolve so as to deal with those from across cultures in a substantial and collaborative way. As such, social science education on cross-cultural processes is critical for people in the modern world. In our modern, globalized world, education regarding the nature of culture is essential!

# Cross-Cultural Psychology

Going back to the 1980s, psychologists began to realize that psychological processes need to be studied in a cultural context (see Hofstede, 1980). This field has expanded extensively in the past several decades and is now the focus of classes at the undergraduate and graduate levels across the nation. With a focus on the culture–psychology interface, this field puts the importance of culture front and center when it comes to the study of the mind and behavior.

In the language of cultural psychology, psychological concepts can be conceptualized as *emics* (which are psychological concepts that are unique to particular cultures) or as *etics*, which are psychological concepts that cut across multiple cultures (see Kitayama & Cohen, 2010). So in an Orthodox Jewish community, an emic might pertain to the specialized manner of washing one's hands before eating a meal during a religious holiday. But the tendency to share a meal together as a celebration would be more of an etic.

The concepts of emic and etic, which are in many ways at the core of cultural psychology, can help us think broadly about the culture–psychology interface. On one hand, all cultures are, by definition, unique and have their own particular way of doing things. On the other hand, when you step back, you can see that all cultures deal with issues that are common to all humans—issues such as relationships, parenting, friendships, cooperation, survival, and death. For these reasons, communication across cultures holds an interesting combination of difference and similarity. When we are dealing with people from cultures that are different from our own, both variation and commonality are always at play.

# Multicultural Counseling

A common theme in this book pertains to the bifurcate worlds of basic and applied psychology. To this point in this chapter, we have been focusing on basic scientific concepts and findings related to the psychology of culture. But, as discussed earlier, students of psychology so often have applied interests. How does cross-cultural psychology work in the real world of applied psychology?

Although there are, in fact, many ways that cultural psychology interfaces with applied psychology. One of the largest such areas is found in *multicultural counseling* (see Sue & Sue, 2016).

Conceptions about issues of mental health and therapy vary wildly across cultural groups. Although some cultures see mental health issues as equivalent to physical health issues by employing the "medical model" of mental health, others see mental health issues as related to spirituality, seeing atypical behavior as related to actions of supernatural elements (see Sue & Sue, 2016). Further, cultures vary from one another in several critically important ways that ultimately pertain to how to best treat issues of behavior and mental health.

For instance, cultures have been found to vary from one another in terms of how *collectivistic* or *individualistic* they are (Triandis, 1995). Individualistic cultures, as found predominantly in the United States, focus on individuals as primary agents. In an individualistic culture, you might be taught to "stand up for yourself" from an early age. In collectivist cultures, as is found in China and many other Asian countries, individuals are taught from an early age to see themselves as part of a broader collective or group. As such, growing up in such a culture, one might be taught that "the nail that stands out gets hammered down" from an early age.

Counseling someone who comes from a strong individualist background requires an entirely different set of concepts and techniques compared with counseling someone from a collectivistic background, for various reasons. Someone from an individualistic culture, for instance, might experience public failure to achieve a goal (such as losing a contest for elected office) as a reason to take pride in one's effort. On the other hand, someone from a collectivistic culture who experiences the same outcome might respond with emotional angst and a belief that he or she has let down his or her whole family.

When it comes to areas of applied psychology, such as mental health counseling, an understanding of culture matters.

## Human Universals

Although culture is, without question, an important concept to keep in mind in studying human psychology, it is similarly important to appreciate and understand that there are many universals that underlie human behavior as well. The field of evolutionary psychology (see Geher, 2014) largely focuses on our shared evolutionary history and on the nature of human universals in behavior and psychological processes.

Human behavior is a funny thing. On one hand, we tend to see wild fluctuations in behavior across different cultures. On the other hand, we all know, at some level, that people are people wherever you go. So, for instance, humans may vary across cultures in terms of how emotionally expressive they are (for instance, with people in the United States being more emotionally expressive than are people in Japan; see Kitayama & Cohen, 2010). However, the emotion system is a basic part of the human experience, and emotional states are expressed by the same facial expressions across all human cultures that have ever been studied.

Let's consider a foundational aspect of what it means to be human: *religion*. In fact, in all cultures that have ever been studied, some kind of religious ideology has been documented (see Wilson, 2002). Further, religious sects vary from one another famously in lots of ways. Most Jews celebrate Sabbath on Saturdays, they do not eat pork, and they engage in prayer in the ancient language of Hebrew. Christians celebrate Sabbath on Sundays, do not have the same laws against pork, and pray in a variety of languages across the globe. Muslims have a different set of practices altogether. And so on.

In a large-scale analysis of more than 100 religions across the globe, renowned evolutionary biologist David Sloan Wilson documented an extraordinary amount of variability in practices and activities associated with the various religions. This said, in using an evolutionary framework, he also found an extraordinary amount of overlap, particularly in terms of the ultimate function of religion across all of these groups. All religions that he studied had two basic elements: (a) some connection with the supernatural (either God or a set of gods, for instance) and (b) a set of policies, rules, or laws designed to get people to engage in self-sacrificing behaviors and to take an approach that focuses on the good of the broader group. So while Judaism and Christianity might differ in terms of a detail such as the appropriate day of the week to celebrate the Sabbath, they both have codes, behavioral norms, and practices that discourage selfish behaviors and that encourage altruistic, other-oriented behaviors. And that ends up being true of all religions that have been studied.

Once you start to consider our evolutionary heritage, culture becomes even more complex. Work in the field of the evolutionary behavioral sciences has a large focus on deep commonalities that exist across seemingly disparate cultures. So, while we need to understand and appreciate the effects of culture on human behavior, we also need to keep an eye on our evolutionary history and consider what all people across the world have in common with one another.

# Where You'll Find Cross-Cultural Psychology in Your Coursework

In addition to having culture be integrated into classes across the curriculum, there are definitely specific courses that will be found in the psychology major that deal with issues of diversity, culture, and behavioral universals in a head-on way. Such classes will typically include the following:

- *Cross-Cultural Psychology*: This course, which is increasingly emerging in undergraduate psychology curricula across the nation, presents students with various frameworks for thinking about the culture/psychology interface.
- *Evolutionary Psychology*: This course is also increasingly emerging in curricula across psychology programs in recent years (see Kruger, Fisher, Platek, & Salmon, 2012). Dedicated to understanding how our evolutionary roots shape behavior, this course has a large focus on (a) human universals in behavior as well as (b) how cultural and genetic influences interact to shape behavioral outcomes.
- *Social Psychology*: A classic course in any psychology curriculum, this course has content dedicated to (a) cultural effects on social behavior as well as (b) social psychological processes that shape how people behave toward members of cultures other than their own.
- *Developmental Psychology*: This course, which is often broken into subcourses (such as *Psychology of Infancy and Childhood*), explores how development across one's life span in a particular environmental context comes to shape behavioral propensities. Given the importance of culture in determining the nature of environmental contexts, developmental psychologists often put a large emphasis on the effects of culture.

- *Personality Psychology*: This course is dedicated to ways that people vary from one another, which is why it is often titled *Individual Differences* at many universities. Given this emphasis on individual differences, it is regular practice for courses in this field to have entire sections dedicated to the influence of culture on behavior. Courses in this field typically include sections dedicated to biological influences, including evolutionary influences, as well.

You will notice in Table 3.1 that *Study Abroad* is included as an option in the *Field Experience* section of the sample curriculum. While taking classes in such areas as cross-cultural psychology and evolutionary psychology is a great thing, no learning experience compares with roll-up-your-sleeves hands-on experiences. Studying abroad during your collegiate experience is a study in cross-cultural psychology sine qua non (which is a Latin phrase meaning "essential").

In fact, the importance of studying abroad has become so central in recent years that colleges and universities across the nation have been growing their international programs, including study abroad experiences. The world is becoming more and more globalized every day, and for so many reasons, studying abroad is becoming an increasingly valuable experience. And schools are going out of their way to provide these kinds of experiences, making sure that they do not impede progress toward graduation. Moreover, study abroad is becoming more accessible for students with financial and health or mobility barriers. In addition to checking out databases of study abroad scholarships (for example, on the website of NAFSA: National Association for Foreign Student Affairs, formerly the National Association of Foreign Student Advisers: https://www.nafsa.org), you can ask in your study abroad and financial aid offices about the possibility of transferring your tuition scholarship to an international program. You can also learn about special partnerships your school might have, such as Generation Study Abroad (http://www.iie.org).

Studying abroad as a psychology student can have all kinds of benefits. For instance, a student who is interested in child development might find parenting and education systems to be very different in a host country, providing new ways to think about psychological development. A student who is interested in an applied career related to psychology might find that the system for mental health care is dramatically different in one's host country compared with one's home. And there may be ways of thinking about the topic of mental health that the student had never been exposed to in his or her curriculum back home. The possibilities for learning in a study abroad context are, in fact, endless!

# The Bottom Line

The world is full of cultural diversity, including all kinds of groups of people with unique norms and approaches to behavior. On the basis of findings from the field of social psychology, we can come to understand why it is inherently difficult for people to comprehend and appreciate the perspectives of those from cultures other than their own. This said, in a world that is becoming increasingly globalized each day, it is critical that we understand cultural processes as they relate to psychological experiences.

At the same time, we must not lose sight of the fact that people truly are people wherever you go and that human universals do exist in populations across the world. So there is a fine balance between cultural variability and behavioral universality. During your undergraduate career you'll explore these issues in detail, working toward the goal of having a deep understanding of the interface between culture and behavior.

# Multifactorial Causation of Behavior

## A Fact of Psychology

5

People like simple explanations of things. We like to believe that World War II happened, for instance, because Hitler was evil. We like to believe that the economic recession that started in 2008 took place because there were unscrupulous bankers on Wall Street. We like to think that the American Revolution took place because the British government was taxing our tea. Sure, in each of these cases the preferred explanation (for example, Hitler's inherently evil nature) played some role in the outcome. But life is complex. And human behavior is complex. And if you learn one thing in college about the nature of human behavior, it should be this: Nearly all human behavior is caused by a variety of variables—variables that may overlap or covary with other variables, often in a complex way. By addressing the fact of multifactorial causation of behavior, this chapter continues our deep dive into the knowledge base of psychology, Goal 1 from the American Psychological Association's (APA's; 2013) *APA Guidelines for the Undergraduate Psychology Major*.

The topic of mass shootings, which has emerged as a major issue in the current environment of the United States, serves as a prototypical example of the kind of psychological phenomenon that clearly is caused by multiple factors. Further, it seems that many people are hesitant to acknowledge the multifactorial nature of mass shootings. People often like to see complex behavioral outcomes, such as mass shootings, as having singular causes. Therefore, some people argue that mass shootings are the result of "mental

http://dx.doi.org/10.1037/0000127-005
*Own Your Psychology Major! A Guide to Student Success*, by G. Geher

health problems"—and nothing else. Others argue that gun availability is the only cause of mass shootings.

Of course, in reality, any mass shooting, as is the case with any complex human behavioral outcome, is caused by multiple factors. To put a face to this concept, consider the tragic mass shooting that left 49 dead and 53 others wounded on June 12, 2016, at the Pulse nightclub in Orlando, Florida. Immediately after the attack, perpetrated by a 29-year-old security guard, people around the world started trying to make sense of it. And, as often happens with human social perception, disagreement over "the cause" of this event emerged across the Internet.

# What Caused the Mass Shooting in Orlando?

Like so many others, I was horrified and disgusted by the Pulse nightclub shooting. An incident like that, which challenges our beliefs that we live in a safe place and that most people are generally "good," shakes us at the heart of who we are.

Behavioral scientists, like myself, are particularly positioned to ask and address questions about such extreme acts of human behavior. Although I am sympathetic to people who believe that they are onto the ultimate cause of what happened (some say *homophobia and intolerance*; some say *religious radicalism*, etc.), I also know that it's important to appreciate the fact of *multifactorial causation* when analyzing this situation that has foisted itself into our collective consciousness.

Multifactorial causation is a truly foundational concept—and it's one that, in my experience, seems not to come naturally to people. So, let's examine it as it applies to a real-world incident.

## "HOMOPHOBIA CAUSED THE ORLANDO SHOOTINGS"

Homophobia is a major issue in the world, and its existence has been documented (to varying degrees) on a global scale (see Vu, Tun, Sheehy, & Nel, 2012). Given all the evidence to date, it seems unlikely that the victims and the venue for the Orlando shootings (which was a known gay nightclub) were unrelated to disturbed levels of homophobia. In fact, the killer was known as explicitly antigay, according to news accounts.

Did the Orlando shootings have something to do with homophobia and discrimination coupled with hate toward the lesbian, gay, bisexual, transgender, and queer community? Yes. This much is clear. This said, homophobia was not the only cause of this tragic event.

## "RADICAL RELIGIOUS ZEALOTRY CAUSED THE ORLANDO SHOOTINGS"

There is no doubt that, despite many benefits, religion has a dark side (see Wilson, 2002). From the Spanish Inquisition to the Holocaust to September 11, millions upon millions of innocent people throughout human history have died in the name of religion. And all the evidence on the Orlando shootings suggests that religious zealotry was certainly not unrelated to what transpired in Orlando. The killer had been on a watchlist for years due to connections with radical Islamist groups. The killer declared, in multiple communications, his allegiance to the Islamic states of Iraq and Syria—and he clearly seemed to, in a highly disturbed line of thinking, believe that he was doing something for the good of God. Of course, this is sickening to think about. But it seems naive to say that his convoluted dedication to his religious beliefs was somehow unrelated to his actions.

Did the Orlando shootings have something to do with radical religious zealotry? You bet.

## "GUN POLICIES CAUSED THE ORLANDO SHOOTINGS"

A lot of people expressed concern about the large-scale pointing of fingers to the National Rifle Association and the gun lobby in regard to the Orlando shootings during what should be, as they indicate, a time of mourning. And it is true that progun individuals say that "*people* kill people." OK. This said, the United States has famously unique gun laws (see Bogus, 1998) that allow individuals to legally purchase powerful weapons like the AR-15 that was used in the Orlando shootings (and that was purchased legally a few days before the incident). Obviously, if the killer had not been able to acquire that weapon, the event would have played out differently. To say that gun laws are somehow unrelated to what happened in Orlando is naive.

Did the Orlando shootings have something to do with gun laws in the United States? It did.

## OTHER CAUSES OF THE ORLANDO SHOOTINGS

Can we come up with other causes of the Orlando shootings, besides the three I have pointed out here? Sure. We can note that the killer was a young male and therefore fits into a group of humans who are more likely to engage in random acts of violence compared with members of other groups. Perhaps he had a troubled upbringing. He may well have experienced trauma in his life. He may well have spent countless hours playing video games that revolve around killing others with guns.

## SOLUTIONS MUST BE MULTIFACTORIAL TOO

The Orlando shootings of June 12, 2016, will go down as a deeply disturbing moment in U.S. history. Forty-nine people died. Their stories have emerged and broken hearts of people around the world. They were individuals. They were parents. They were sons. They were daughters. They were spouses. They were brothers. They were sisters. And they are now gone—and we are left trying to figure out why.

The process of understanding how this incident could have happened is disturbing. While people gravitate toward unifactorial explanations of complex behavior—once you think about it, it's clear that the Orlando shooting, like any complex human behavioral event, has multiple causes. And any work by behavioral scientists looking to make sure that such events are less likely to take place in the future, for the good of our children, will be wise to take a multifactorial approach.

In fact, the concept of multifactorial causation is, to my mind, one of the single most important ideas that students need to learn during their educational career as a psychology student. This one is big!

# The Concentric Circle Approach to Understanding Psychological Complexity

Renowned developmental psychologist Urie Bronfenbrenner was very attuned to the idea of multifactorial causation when it comes to causes that surround behavior. In a 1977 article in *American Psychologist*, later developed visually as a set of concentric or nested circles (i.e., circles within circles), Bronfenbrenner articulated a model for how some causes of behavior across development take place close to the individual or even within the individual (such as physiological factors that underlie behavior like hormones), while other causes of one's behavior are more remote from the person him or herself (such as the culture in which one is raised).

For the purposes of advancing the concept of multifactorial causation, I have adapted Bronfenbrenner's concentric circle approach to provide a model of how factors that underlie behavior exist at levels that vary from each other in terms of how close or distant they are to the individual. This model, which serves as the intellectual basis for the remainder of the chapter, is presented in Figure 5.1.

As you can see in this model, the "close-in" factors near the center of the figure include such concepts as genetic and physiological causes of behavior. As we move outward, we encounter factors that are also either inside the person, such as dispositional traits, or that are in the immediate environment of one's upbringing, such as one's learning history and developmental experiences. As we move further out again, we encounter situational factors, moving on to the large-scale factors of culture and evolutionary history. Interestingly, psychologists ask questions about behavior that cut across this entire model. The remainder of this chapter describes and provides examples of these various classes of behavioral causes in action.

## GENETIC CAUSES OF BEHAVIOR

So let's start with two simple questions: Why do people cheat in relationships? Why does infidelity exist? Well at this point in the chapter, you are likely (rightfully) thinking that there are all kinds of factors involved. People may, in fact, cheat in relationships for reasons such as the following:

- They are unhappy in their current relationship.
- Cheating is the norm in their friend group, and they are following suit.
- They go out to wild parties where people hook up all the time.
- They were raised in unstable conditions and have come to rely on a variety of sexual relationships to help boost self-esteem.

**FIGURE 5.1**

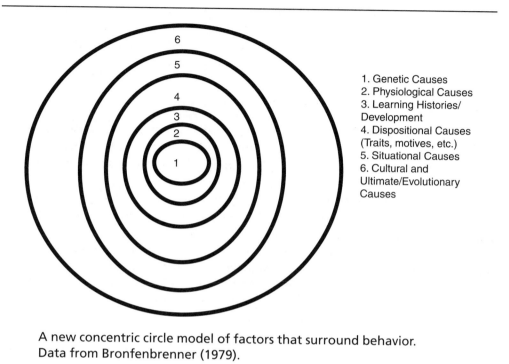

1. Genetic Causes
2. Physiological Causes
3. Learning Histories/
Development
4. Dispositional Causes
(Traits, motives, etc.)
5. Situational Causes
6. Cultural and
Ultimate/Evolutionary
Causes

A new concentric circle model of factors that surround behavior.
Data from Bronfenbrenner (1979).

And those are just for starters. One reason that you may not have come up with is this: Maybe cheating is in one's genes. Maybe people with certain genetic combinations are more likely to engage in infidelity than are others.

In a study published in 2010, Justin Garcia and his colleagues examined the behavioral correlates of a particular variant of a gene referred to as the *DRD4* gene. This gene comes in multiple varieties. In some people, the pattern is elongated across the chromosome, repeating multiple times. In a subset of people, the pattern, in fact, repeats seven or more times. In others, it is essentially shorter. And get this: The length of one's *DRD4* variant is easily observed based on an analysis of one's saliva.

As the longer variant of this gene had been documented as being associated with a battery of risk-related behaviors in social contexts, the researchers hypothesized that people with the longer variants of this gene would be more likely to report having engaged in sexual infidelity. And that is exactly what they found. In fact, individuals in the 7+ condition (i.e., who had the pattern repeat seven or more times in their particular genome) were about 50% more likely than were others to have engaged in sexual infidelity.

The relationship between genes and behavior is a complex one to be sure. Genes do not control the nervous system. Rather, they code for protein synthesis that oversees the production of physiological structures that do, ultimately, constitute the nervous system (and other systems in our bodies). So we need to realize that the relationship between genes and behavior is highly indirect and complex. This said, studies such as this one by Garcia et al. (2010) make it clear that, in an important way, genes do shape important behavioral outcomes in humans.

## PHYSIOLOGICAL CAUSES OF BEHAVIOR

Stepping toward the outer circle, we next consider physiological causes of behavior. These are behaviors that are still "close in." These are causes of behavior that are essentially embedded in one's physiology—factors that shape behavior in important ways.

There are several kinds of physiological factors that shape behavior. For instance, chemical signals in the brain, referred to as *neurotransmitters*, play an important role in behavior. The variety in the kinds of neurons that exist, including neurons responsible for taking information in from the external world and then for producing bodily reactions (*afferent* and *efferent neurons*), plays a role in shaping behavior. Further, hormones of various kinds have been found to shape behavior as well.

Want an interesting finding regarding the effects of hormones on behavior? Well, regardless of what you answered, here it is!

In 2007, a highly cited and highly publicized study by researchers at the University of New Mexico was published in the journal *Evolution and Human Behavior*. Miller, Tybur, and Jordan (2007) explored the effects of estradiol (a female hormone that varies across the ovulatory cycle) and the amount of money made in tips by female strippers at a nightclub.

The researchers predicted that women who were near peak ovulation, and thus higher in estradiol levels, would more effectively engage in sexy behavior in their roles and would, therefore, receive higher tips compared with women who were at other points in their cycles. And this is exactly what the researchers found. In fact, within a woman's own experience, a particular female dancer made more tips, on average, when she was near peak ovulation compared with when she was at other times in her cycle.

As is the case with the effects of genes on behavior, the effects of hormones on behavior follow a complex pathway. It turns out that changes in hormone levels catalyze various features of our psychology, having effects that are social, emotional, and behavioral in nature.

In any case, from this study by Miller et al. (2007), we can see that internal physiological factors shape outward behavior—and even important outcomes such as amount of monetary gain.

## DEVELOPMENTAL CAUSES OF BEHAVIOR

Moving slightly toward the outer circles, we have developmental causes of behavior. Think about the last time that you had an all-out temper tantrum, crying and kicking and screaming, throwing things on the floor. You may have had one in the past year or so (it happens!), but odds are it was a while back. You may have been 7 years old.

One important factor that underlies behavior, across all other contexts, pertains to developmental stage. In another words, a major reason people do what they do is found in simply understanding their life stage. If a 3-year-old throws a temper tantrum, that is par for the course. If a 33-year-old throws a temper tantrum, that is something else altogether.

If a teenager paints his nails black, pierces his face, and wears a T-shirt of some new heavy metal group from England, we say that he is going through a phase. This is considered part of normal development, when adolescents try on various identities as they essentially try to "find themselves" (see Marcia, 1966). If a 47-year-old lawyer comes to work dressed in this same way, people would likely whisper around the office that something is not right!

Life stage famously affects behavior and psychological processes—and this starts in the prenatal phase. Many psychologists, such as Jean Piaget, focused their entire careers on studying and understanding the specific ways that young children see and interact with the world, along with stages that they seem to pass through during psychological development. Suffice it to say, development matters: Development is a major context, across any and all other factors, that profoundly influences behavior.

## THE IMPORTANCE OF LEARNING

In the field of psychology, *learning* has a pretty specific meaning. When I took a class in the psychology of learning as an undergraduate years ago, I was surprised at how technical the class was and by how little it dealt with educational processes. In fact, in the field of psychology, *learning* goes hand in hand with the field of *behaviorism* (see Skinner, 1981). The field of behaviorism, and its modern counterpart *applied behavior analysis*, focuses on our unique learning histories as major causes of our behavior. Through such learning mechanisms as *classical conditioning* (when animals come to associate multiple stimuli with one another that are regularly paired in its environment) and *operant conditioning* (when animals come to pair their responses with some outcomes that systematically follow from the responses), behavior becomes *shaped*, and we tend to emit shaped behavior based on our learning histories.

To understand how one's learning history plays an important role in one's behavior, consider a child who is hesitant to engage in creative activities, getting anxious when asked to draw a picture or to sing a song. This behavioral characterization might follow from that child not having been rewarded for engaging in creative tasks in the past. If the child's efforts to do something novel or to do something creative have not been rewarded across his or her learning history (either within the household or at school), then that child's behavior will be shaped as such. Creative behaviors will become less of a part of that child's *behavioral repertoire*, and that child may end up choosing activities in school and beyond that do not have a creative component.

Importantly, learning processes such as classical and operant conditioning shape behavior not just of children, but of all people. The groundbreaking work of behaviorists such as B. F. Skinner have shed light on such areas of functioning as

- gambling,
- drug addiction,
- sexual behaviors,
- education,
- anxiety and depression,
- schizophrenia,

and more.

Further, learning processes, as Skinner (1981) himself rightfully pointed out, are largely universal across a broad array of animal species, and the concepts developed by the behaviorists have led to the primary techniques that are now used in training all kinds of animals—from dogs and pigs to pigeons and goldfish. And yes, even cats!

One reason we do what we do is found in our own unique learning histories. We have been rewarded for some behaviors and punished for others. Simply put: We are more likely to engage in behaviors that have been rewarded in the past.

## DISPOSITIONAL CAUSES OF BEHAVIOR

As observers of the behaviors of others, or as "lay observers" (see Ross & Nisbett, 1991), people tend to see the causes of the behaviors of others as residing inside of those others. This bias, referred to as the *fundamental attribution error* (see Ross, 1977), essentially suggests that people in general (as opposed to scientific psychologists) tend to see such internal features as personality traits as the causes of behaviors of others.

For instance, if you see someone ahead of you driving in traffic, tailgating and passing other cars left and right, you might think, "That guy is a jerk!"—that he is impatient and rude. Well, it may well be that he (or she!) is impatient and rude; but other explanations may account for what is going on. For instance, it might be a pregnant woman driving—one who is all alone and whose water just broke. Or maybe it is a young couple with a dog—a dog that just got hit by a car and that desperately needs medical attention. The fact is that when we see others behave, our tendency to "blame the person for his or her behavior" is not always right.

In fact, the entire issue of how much personality variables shape behavior is one of the hotly contested debates in the field of psychology proper. Personality psychologists tend to argue that internal, dispositional traits do, in fact, account for behavior in a substantial and important way (see Gosling, Rentfrow, & Swann, 2003). One of the great successes of personality psychology is the development of the *Big Five* model of personality psychology (see Costa & McCrae, 1985; Gosling et al., 2003). After decades of research into the basic structure of human personality, personality psychologists have come to determine that pretty much all personality traits that exist map onto one of five basic dimensions of personality—dimensions that have been found to characterize human personality in populations across the globe. These Big Five dimensions are

- Extraversion (how outgoing someone is),
- Emotional stability (how emotionally stable someone is),
- Agreeableness (how much one tends to go with the flow and agree with others),
- Openness (how open-minded one is to new ideas), and
- Conscientiousness (how diligent and reliable one is across a variety of tasks).

Importantly, these five dimensions are just that: dimensions! They are not categories. It's not like someone either is an extravert or is not. Rather, these dimensions are conceptualized as continuous, with most people scoring about average on them and some scoring "high" and some scoring "low." This is an important point because many people misunderstand personality dimensions as personality categories, which they are not. So each person scores somewhere along a continuum on each trait dimension.

Researchers using the Big Five and other modern models of personality have found that valid measures of personality traits do, in fact, provide an important basis for predicting all kinds of behavior (see Larsen & Buss, 2013). For instance, scores for emotional stability tend to be predictive of success in intimate relationships, depressive tendencies, and problems in one's social world (see Geher & Wedberg, 2019).

So if you want to know why people do what they do, you need to understand personality traits that drive their behaviors in regular ways.

## SITUATIONAL CAUSES OF BEHAVIOR

Although dispositional factors do play a role in shaping behaviors, social psychologists have famously shown how situational factors often play an even more important one here—often surprisingly so.

### Situational Factors and Obedience to Authority

Perhaps the best-known study that shows the impact of immediate situational factors on behavior is the classic study of obedience to authority conducted by Yale University's Stanley Milgram (1963). Essentially, what Milgram's study revealed is that most "regular" people are capable of obeying an authority figure's commands, even, as you will soon see, to the point of killing an innocent other.

Milgram's (1963) work, arguably the most highly cited and most important research in the history of the social sciences, involved having groups of adults take on the role of "teacher" in a laboratory experiment. In this experiment (which included much in the way of deception about the true purpose of the study), the "teacher" was told to administer electric shocks to a "learner" (actually an actor who was working with the researcher) who was also a participant in the study. The shocks were to increase each time the "learner" made a mistake, and the machine used to administer these shocks (which were actually fake) was labeled with such terms as "DANGER" and "XXX." Further, the experimenter, a tall, serious guy in a lab coat, told the "teacher" that he or she must continue increasing the voltage. Then the "learner" would start screaming and complain of a heart condition. After the voltages reached extremely high levels, however, the "learner" stopped responding in any capacity at all.

In short, this drama (filled with deception that would probably not pass reviews of modern-day ethics boards, by the way) was designed to get the real participants (the "teachers") to think that they had just killed another human. The questions being studied were: (a) At what point will participants choose to disobey the experimenter telling them to administer the shocks? and (b) What conditions would make participants more or less likely to disobey the experimenter? (Milgram, 1963).

Milgram's research is certainly a high point in the semester for any social psychology class. The lessons learned and the power of the study itself combine for a deep and important lesson on the nature of human behavior.

Importantly, Milgram studied a host of dispositional factors as they related to obedience. He and his research assistants collected data on age and gender and evaluated various personality traits based on measures that were available at the time. Relevant to the current conversation, it was interesting to see that the personality variables had little effect on people's obedience. Rather, manipulations of situational factors seemed to play a much larger role in determining whether people would obey the authority. For example, if the participants who had to administer shocks could see the experimenter but could not see the "learner" receiving the (fake) shocks, they would increase the voltage all the way to the 450-volt mark on the machine.

An important implication of Milgram's research from the perspective of psychology is this: Perhaps our behavior is more under the control of factors that are in our immediate situations rather than by factors that are stamped into our personalities.

## My Favorite Psychology Study

This discussion regarding the person and the situation brings me to my all-time favorite psychology study, which has enormous implications for understanding the topic of multifactorial causation and for understanding why people do what they do.

### Setting

Early 1970s, campus of Princeton University in New Jersey.

Two behavioral scientists, John Darley and Daniel Batson (1973), were interested in studying the psychology of prosocial behavior. Why do people do good things for others?

### Method

To examine this question, they decided to study students at the Princeton Theological Seminary—in other words, Princeton students who were studying to be church leaders. At the risk of stereotyping (remember outgroup homogeneity?), you kind of figure that these folks should have the concept of goodness down!

The basic point of the study was to see whether dispositional or situational factors are more influential in determining prosocial behavior. In other words, when someone is kind to another, is this because he or she has some innate qualities within that lead to kindness—or because some situational factors simply determine and allow for kind behaviors.

So these researchers set up an epic study. Across 3 days in late autumn, they had a bunch of seminary students come to a building, meet with a researcher, and fill out various surveys. The surveys partly addressed whether the students were religious primarily for intrinsic or for extrinsic reasons (with *intrinsic reasons* being factors such as "I am motivated to do good in the world" and *extrinsic reasons* being factors such as "I really want to get into Heaven"). Then the participants were told that they needed to prepare a brief talk about the Good Samaritan from the Bible—which is a story about how a hapless victim on the side of the road was just passed by from a bunch of holy individuals—while a nonholy Samaritan took the time to stop and help the fellow out. The content of the story becomes relevant, as you'll see.

Participants were all told that they needed to walk to a nearby building to meet up with another member of the team and then to give their sermon. They then, by random chance, were determined to be in one of three conditions. They were told that they

1. had plenty of time and were early,
2. were on time but should head over now so as not to be late, or
3. were running late and really needed to skedaddle.

Then comes the fun part. The situation was rigged; all participants found a fallen stranger in a narrow alleyway. The "stranger" was really a confederate of the researchers, and his role was to seem sick on the ground and in need of help. The catch was that the alleyway was only 4 feet across—so to not help this guy, you had to step over him!

## Results

I learned about this study around 1995, and its lessons have shaped my approach to life ever since. Here are the essential findings: Dispositional factors had no bearing on helping behavior. In other words, people who reported being religious for intrinsic reasons were no more likely than others were to stop to help. On the other hand, the "time-constraint" variable mattered a ton:

- 63% of participants in the "early" condition stopped to help the stranger.
- 45% of participants in the "on time" condition stopped to help the stranger.
- 10% of participants in the "late" condition stopped to help the stranger.

## Lessons of the Good Samaritan Study

This study has dramatic implications for what it means to be human. First off, the overall amount of "helping" was low—with most (60% of) participants actually being *unwilling* to help the "victim." This is, of course, ironic, because the participants were

1. Princeton students studying to be Christian leaders and
2. about to give a talk on the lessons of the Good Samaritan from the Bible!

And that's not all! The participants who claimed that they were interested in working in the clergy for intrinsic reasons, because they felt a strong motive to help others, were no more likely to actually stop and help the victim than were other participants.

On top of this, it turns out that simple-seeming situational factors—whether one was in a hurry or not—played the dominant role in determining what that person would do.

When it comes to human behavior, we have a strong bias toward thinking that people do what they do because of internal traits that drive their behaviors (see Ross & Nisbett, 1991). Don't be fooled by this general social-perceptual tendency. In reality, dispositional factors may be relatively weak predictors of what we do, and situational factors, which often seem benign or inconsequential, play powerful roles in shaping our behaviors.

## CULTURAL CAUSES OF BEHAVIOR

As we move toward the outer rings of our concentric circles (from Figure 5.1), we move toward factors that shape behavior in less direct kinds of ways than do factors in the inner circles. Culture, as we discussed in detail in Chapter 4, is precisely this kind of larger context that surrounds behavior. As we have already discussed, culture has a powerful, but indirect, influence on all facets of behavior (see Kitayama & Cohen, 2010). I'll explicate this point with an anecdote.

My wife, Kathy, oversees an international program on our campus. In her program, students from Turkey spend several semesters at the State University of New York (SUNY) New Paltz taking classes and developing their understanding of our culture and language. When the program first started in about 2005, there were some growing pains. Turkish culture differs considerably from culture in the United States, and some issues needed to be addressed. For instance, Kathy got a complaint one day from the administrators on campus who oversee dormitory life for students: Apparently the Turkish students were not putting their trays away in the dining hall. Rather, they were leaving the trays on the tables and walking out. Not surprisingly, the students from the United States considered this rude, as did the staff in the dining hall.

So, being a good academic administrator, Kathy met with several of the students to get to the bottom of it. Well, get this: Apparently in Turkey, it is considered rude to put your dishes away in a public place such as a dining hall. People are paid to do that work in Turkey, and doing that work for them is considered an insult. Ha! So there you have an instance of a behavior that may have seemed like it was caused by personality features (selfish, lazy, etc.) but was actually shaped by cultural factors.

I have gotten to know many Turkish individuals through Kathy's program and through other spheres of my academic work; some of these people are the brightest and kindest people I have ever met in my life. I consider myself privileged to have them in my life. This said, let me provide one more anecdote about the influence of culture on behavior before moving ahead. In trying to get her Turkish students the best possible and most holistic experience while they are here in the United States, she often books extracurricular experiences for them. One year, she booked a bus to an amusement park that was about 90 minutes north of us. There was room on the bus for me, along with our two kids. We were planning on some fun!

The students on the bus were not all Turkish. Several Japanese students, also studying at New Paltz, joined the trip. After the bus stopped, people got off and got in line to get their tickets for the amusement park. I will never forget how that played out!

About half of the students on the bus were Turkish, and about half were Japanese. Well, Turkish students can be pretty bold (hence the phrase "young Turk"), and in their culture there is a set of norms regarding speaking up for yourself and making sure that you get your fair share. Japan is the exact opposite. In highly collectivistic Japan, people are raised to defer to others and to put the interests of others ahead of their own. Long story short: I was amused to see that every single Turkish student made it into the line ahead of every single Japanese student—there were zero exceptions! As a result, the Turks got their tickets first and entered the park first, not surprisingly. And everyone had a great time!

In any case, an understanding of the psychology of culture, of course, puts this in perspective. Cultural factors affect our behavior at every step, often beyond our own awareness of this being the case.

## EVOLUTIONARY CAUSES OF BEHAVIOR

Also near the outer of the concentric circles, we find evolutionary factors that shape behavior. In fact, evolution-based factors can be so distant in terms of how they are causing behavior that they may actually be the result of experiences from millions of years ago—and on another continent!

Evolutionary psychologists (see Geher, 2014) see human behavior as the product of evolutionary forces such as natural selection. The basic idea is that under ancestral conditions, some behavioral patterns (which had some heritable or genetic component) were more likely than other patterns to lead to survival or reproduction. Such patterns that were more likely to lead to survival and/or reproduction were considered *adaptive*. An evolutionary account of a behavioral pattern, then, suggests that the cause of the behavior may be buried millions of generations deep in our heritage as a species.

Consider, for instance, fear of snakes (see Öhman & Mineka, 2001). Fear of snakes is a common fear among modern humans, even though most of us rarely see snakes in our day-to-day lives. Interestingly, people are more likely to show fear reactions to snakes than to guns or electrical outlets, which are stimuli that actually pose more likely dangers to those of us who live in industrialized conditions.

So why would modern people fear snakes so much? From an evolutionary perspective, the answer is simple: Under ancestral conditions, during the lion's share of human evolutionary history in the African savanna, snakes were common, and we have good reason to believe that death by snake by was common. As such, developing a fear of snakes would make good adaptive and evolutionary sense. Those of our ancestors who happened to naturally have such a fear were more likely to avoid snakes—and thus to survive, passing on an inherited propensity to fear snakes.

Why might someone today show a fear response to a snake? The answer is largely found in the fact that this person's ancestors, thousands of generations back, were selected by nature to have a natural fear of snakes. Now *that* is a distant explanation that is definitely in the outer rings of the concentric circles!

## The Bottom Line

When it comes to understanding human psychology, the concept of multifactorial causation is essential. As explicated by the concentric-circle model presented early in the chapter, factors that shape behavior exist at multiple levels, including *proximate* levels (such as specific genes or physiological processes), *intermediate* levels (such as personality traits or situational factors), and *ultimate* levels (such as large-scale cultural and evolutionary factors).

When it comes to any particular behavioral outcome, there is never a single factor that accounts for it. In fact, behavior is always the result of a complex interplay of factors, including factors that vary from one another in terms of how close they are to the person at the time of the action.

# SCIENTIFIC INQUIRY AND CRITICAL THINKING III

One thing that often surprises students about the psychology curriculum pertains to the scientific foundation of this field. While people outside the field seem to enjoy debating whether this field "is" or "is not" a scientific discipline (this is standard Thanksgiving conversation during a psychology major's first semester, by the way), within the field itself, there is no such debate. All psychologists conceptualize the field as a scientific area of inquiry.

A *scientific area of inquiry* is some academic area that focuses on explaining and developing methods for predicting some empirical (i.e., observable) phenomena. In the field of psychology, the phenomena of interest are behaviors. And our scientific approaches to understanding, explaining, and predicting behaviors come from (a) the many theoretical concepts that exist in the field (e.g., behaviorism, evolutionary psychology), (b) the formulation of specific hypotheses based on these theoretical concepts, (c) the formal testing of these hypotheses, and (d) statistical analyses to assess the degree to which the different hypotheses were validated by the data.

In the psychology curriculum, the skills you need to be able to conduct each of these features of the research process build on each other to get you to the larger goal of critical thinking and scientific inquiry. The American Psychological Association's (APA's; 2013) *APA Guidelines for the Undergraduate Psychology Major*, Goal 2: Scientific Inquiry and Critical Thinking, includes learning outcomes that address statistics and research methods in psychology. Chapters 6 and 7 cover these topics. Further, many of the skills you'll learn in research methods align with Goal 4: Communication; this is covered in Chapter 7 as well.

## Chapter 6: Psychology Is a Real Science: Part I. The Many Joys of Statistics

This chapter focuses on the mathematical foundation that underlies all of the scientific work in the behavioral sciences: statistics. Even if you don't master every statistical operation that exists during your undergraduate career, just understanding how statistics work at a basic level will help you with a lot of things. First, it will help you digest and comment on existing research findings—in other words, it will give you mental "shelves" where you can better organize what you learn about science. Second, it will help you ask your own questions in such a way that the answers are quantifiable (measurable). And third, you'll be able to use statistics to create a logical process for thinking about a variety of psychological issues.

## Chapter 7: Psychology Is a Real Science: Part II. Research Methods in the Behavioral Sciences

Research methods is the big sister to statistics in most psychology curricula. It is usually considered critical to have some facility with statistics before taking a research methods class. It is in this class that students learn how ask questions about behavior in scientific terms. They also learn the nuts and bolts needed to actually go out and test these questions. In short, you need to learn about research methods so that you think critically about any findings that are presented to you before accepting or rejecting them.

# Psychology Is a Real Science
## Part I. The Many Joys of Statistics

# 6

Those who know me well, know that there are few things in the world I love as much as I love teaching statistics. In the psychology curriculum, statistics is something of a breath of fresh air for me. I think this is partly because there are always correct answers in this particular class. If the answer to a question is 4.95, then that is just the answer! In so many other psychology classes, answers to questions seem like they may be up for debate—largely because psychology is so filled with multiple perspectives on so many topics. But not so for statistics.

This chapter focuses on statistics in a stepped-back kind of way. Rather than presenting you with the nuts and bolts of how to compute the many statistics that we use in our work, the point of this chapter is to provide you with a birds-eye view of this area, including information that will help you understand the significance of this class in the curriculum. After a brief pep talk, we'll get into the learning outcomes that statistics classes will help you fulfill.

## Why You Too Will Love Statistics

Did I mention that I love teaching statistics? Well, then, would you be surprised if I told you that I cowrote a textbook all about statistics? I didn't think so! In our textbook on statistics (Geher & Hall, 2014), we start out

http://dx.doi.org/10.1037/0000127-006
*Own Your Psychology Major! A Guide to Student Success*, by G. Geher

by acknowledging some basic facts that we've learned through experience. We've found there are three primary hurdles to learning statistics. See if you identify with any of these:

1. Students do not want to learn the material.
2. Students do not see the material as relevant to their everyday lives.
3. Students are downright scared by the course.

Thankfully, each of these hurdles is surmountable. Let's briefly address these three hurdles in turn.

## BARRIER 1: NOT WANTING TO LEARN THE MATERIAL

I have to admit, when I was an 18-year-old freshman in college and I opened up my statistics textbook, I was like "Accckkkkk!!!!" So I get it. You might have thought that you were getting out of math and science by taking a major in psychology. If that was the case for you, then the statistics class would understandably give you pause.

So why should you want to learn this material? Well, for one, my students often report that the math of it is easier than they had expected. Typically, the math is no more complicated than is found in a basic algebra class taught to eighth and ninth graders. Once you realize that the math is relatively benign (even if there are many symbols and equations), things change.

Also, you will see that the content of this class is immensely helpful in advancing you through the psychology program and in understanding the world in a new and powerful way.

## BARRIER 2: NOT SEEING THE MATERIAL AS RELEVANT TO YOUR EVERYDAY LIFE

At first glance, I'd say that this tends to be true: Statistics is one of the many important areas of intellectual inquiry that students just don't see as relevant. Well, it is! And once you see this, you'll start to become motivated to learn the material.

To explicate the relevance to everyday life, consider the following questions that you might ask about your own academic world:

- Why is *she* so popular with all of the teachers? What are the characteristics that *she* has that make teachers like her? And do other people with these same qualities also get into the good graces of their teachers?
- In my class on English literature, I have fallen behind on the reading, but I regularly attend all of the lectures and take great notes. Will I do all right on the exam, given this fact?
- Where I go to college, we have a long rainy season that lasts for months on end. I always wonder if attendance in classes is lower at the university during these months.

OK, there you have it. Each of these is the kind of question that you as a student might think about from time to time. What you may not realize, however, is that these are all questions that can be conceptualized in statistical terms. And, in fact, we can design studies and use statistical processes to address each and every one of these questions.

Let's think about that first question: The student who seems to just "have it." What has *she* got?! If you were going to think further about this, you might think about her classroom behavior. Does she sit in the front of the class? Does she ask questions regularly? Does she have strong attendance? And what about outside of the classroom? Does she visit the professor during office hours? And what about her personality? Does Little-Ms.-Teacher's-Pet have an extremely extroverted personality? Is she not just friendly but, perhaps, super friendly?

Now suppose that the answer was "yes" to each and every one of these questions. A statistically minded approach would be, then, to try to tease apart the influence of each of these different characteristics. In other words, of each of these qualities that we have determined is held by this student, which particular quality or qualities are primarily responsible for getting teachers to like this student? In your statistics class, you will learn about a procedure called *regression analysis*, which will allow you to ask precisely this question.

Now let's think about that second question: This is the one about the student who fell behind in the reading in English literature and is wondering if just studying the notes from the lectures might help carry him on the exam. From a statistical standpoint, we can think about the question this way: Do students who do both the readings and attend lectures score, on average, better than do students who only attend the lectures. We would use a statistical procedure called a *between-groups* t-test to address this kind of question. (But let me give you a spoiler alert: This question is based on my own experience with a course in English literature in 1989. The answer was this: I should have done the reading! I got my only *D* in college in that class, and looking back, I deserved it! You can do better than that!)

Now let's look at that third question: What is the relationship between the weather and attendance at classes in college? More specifically, does attendance at classes on a campus correlate with the amount of precipitation in a day? Do fewer students attend classes, on average, on relatively rainy days compared with relatively dry days? Is the pattern the same whether the campus is mainly residential or mainly commuter? If you go to school in the Pacific Northwest, where I taught for 2 years, then you know what I am talking about!

To address a question like this one, we would use a process called a *correlation analysis*. This kind of analysis seeks to examine whether two variables—here we have (a) amount of precipitation and (b) class attendance—are significantly related to one another. A correlation will not only tell you whether two variables are related, it will also provide you with information on the nature of the direction of the relationship between these variables. It is very useful! The tools that you take away from statistics class can be applied to questions about pretty much anything.

## BARRIER 3: BEING SCARED OF THE COURSE

In my experience, a good proportion of students always seem scared of the statistics course. They will say things on the first day such as

- "I am scared of this class!"
- "I am not good at math!"
- "I have NEVER been good at math!"
- "What if I fail?"

If you are afraid of statistics, don't hesitate to reach out to your instructor and hold him or her responsible for helping you. Odds are that your instructor is in this profession because he or she wants to help people like you develop and reach new levels. Specific advice on this front is as follows:

- *Ask questions in class.* If you don't understand something in your statistics class and you are paying attention, don't hesitate for one second to raise your hand and ask the teacher to explain or reexplain the concept. This is *your* education.
- *See your professor during office hours.* Seeing your professor during office hours has several potential benefits. Doing so will make sure that she or he knows who you are and that you care. It will also give you special opportunities to ask questions and to get feedback on your work.
- *Give 100% of yourself to this class.* As indicated earlier, most of the actual math is no more advanced than eighth-grade algebra. This said, there are a lot of concepts and formulas. And the class is highly *cumulative*. This is to say that the content builds on itself. So missing a class or a homework assignment can really have adverse effects on your ability to succeed in this class. If you do all of the homework assignments to the best of your ability and attend every class meeting (emergencies aside), you really will be set up for success in this course.

# What Will Statistics Help You to Do?

Statistics that are used in psychology come in a few varieties. To understand the nature of the basic statistics that we use in the field, it is important to note that the statistics portion of a psychology major is largely designed to map onto Goal 2 from the American Psychological Association's (APA's; 2013) *APA Guidelines for the Undergraduate Psychology Major*: Scientific Inquiry and Critical Thinking. That goal has five learning outcomes total, but statistics mainly fulfills these two:

2.1 Use scientific reasoning to interpret psychological phenomena
2.2 Demonstrate psychology information literacy

Outcomes 2.3, 2.4, and 2.5 are addressed in Chapter 7. So for now, let's think about how the content of our statistics courses maps onto these *APA Guidelines*.

# Use Scientific Reasoning to Interpret Psychological Phenomena

The main kind of scientific reasoning that we use to interpret psychological phenomena is found in our statistical processes. Suppose that you wanted to interpret whether people were anxious as a result of being told that they had a pop quiz in statistics one day. After telling them that they were about to have a pop quiz, you then give them a measure of anxiety (based on self-reports). The scale for the anxiety measure is 1 to 10 (with 10 meaning *more anxious*). You collect the data, and you need to interpret the findings. You are, per Learning Outcome 2.1, interpreting these psychological phenomena.

What would you do next? Most likely, you would want to see what kinds of scores people obtained on the anxiety measure. That is, you would want to see what the *central tendency* is—or what typical scores were like. What score did most people get (*mode*)? What is the middle score of the range of scores (*median*)? What is the average score (*mean*)? These markers of central tendency, mode, median, and mean, are, in fact standard ways to summarize data in statistics.

In addition to knowing what typical scores are like for a variable (i.e., central tendency), we also are often interested in how much the scores tend to vary from one another (i.e., variability). So imagine, for instance, that on the 1-to-10 anxiety scale, the mean is 8. OK. But how much do the scores vary from one another? Did anyone score a 1? Did everyone score an 8? These are questions of variability that are, like questions of central tendency, foundational in our understanding of statistics in psychology. And as with central tendency, there are multiple ways to statistically track variability. The most common way to do this is via something we call *standard deviation*, which is, approximately, the average amount that scores on some variable vary from one another.

You will see that there are algebraic formulas and processes for computing such statistics as the mean and the standard deviation, and you will learn the nuts and bolts of this in your statistics class. Here, I introduce these concepts so that you have a leg up and have a sense of what these things are all about in the first place.

# Understanding Statistical Significance and Effect Size

With statistics in psychology, there are two basic ways that we discuss whether some finding is a big deal. It's not difficult to find things once you start collecting psychological data. The trick is to find things that are (a) interpretable and (b) worth telling others about. If 100 studies have already found that interrupted sleep tends to predict poor test performance, and then I go ahead and collect data and replicate that result, it's not a bad thing, but it's not necessarily worth alerting the news outlets about it.

With our modern statistical processes, we have two basic ways of discussing if a finding is a big deal or not. We call these *effect size* and *statistical significance*.

## EFFECT SIZE

Effect size literally speaks to how big an effect is. For instance, suppose that you had two groups in the anxiety study we discussed earlier. Members of one group spent an hour in a spa and then completed the anxiety measure. Members of the other group went into stats class and were told that they had a pop quiz. You might imagine that the anxiety score for the students in the spa condition would be, on average, lower than the comparable score in the pop-quiz condition. Fair enough.

Now, to speak to effect size, we would be asking whether the difference is a big difference. We have fancy statistical tools for examining questions of effect size—but let's not forget that the basic question of effect size is quite simple. Is the effect big or not?

To put a face to it, imagine a scenario in which the mean anxiety score for the pop-quiz participants is 8 and the mean for the spa participants is 2. Would you say that this is a big difference? Probably. Again, the actual statistics that are used to calculate these kinds of things are a little more complex, but this is the basic idea. Now compare that with a situation in which the mean for the pop quiz group was 5.5 and the mean for the spa group was 5.4. In this condition would you say that there is a big effect size? Probably not.

So this is the idea of effect size. And it literally means what it is called: Is the effect sizeable? Is it "big?" Is it worth making a big deal about?

## STATISTICAL SIGNIFICANCE

Statistical significance, often represented by the term $p < .05$, has a straightforward meaning. If a finding is said to be statistically significant, it simply means that the pattern of findings found in a study is likely to generalize to the broader population of interest. That. Is. It.

For instance, suppose you did a study with 100 cats and 100 dogs. And you found that, in your sample, 80 of the dogs were able to be trained to go through a hoop compared with only one cat. And suppose you ran some statistical test (such as the between-groups $t$ test) and found that $p < .05$. That would simply mean that the pattern you found, with dogs being better at jumping through hoops, is likely to be a pattern that holds across the entire population of dogs and the entire population of cats. Further, this statistical language implies that the probability of the pattern of findings from the study *not* generalizing to the broader populations of interest is small—less than 5% (thus, $p < .05$)—with $p$ meaning *probability* and .05 simply meaning 5%.

What is magical about 5%? Nothing really. It's kind of a practical benchmark that statisticians have come to use as a standard over years and years and across lots of different disciplines. In fact, there are some conditions in which you will see $p < .01$ or even $p < .001$. These terms simply mean that the likelihood of the finding not generalizing to the broader population of interest is less than 1/100 ($p < .01$) or less than 1/1,000 ($p < .001$).

As we've seen so far, statistics are tools used by psychologists and behavioral scientists. They are designed to be neither scary nor mysterious. They are straightforward mathematical tools designed to help us better understand the world. Statistical significance and its related term $p < .05$ are simple concepts—meaning that the pattern found in a sample likely generalizes to the broader population of interest that is being studied. There's no abracadabra there!

And effect size is a similarly straightforward concept. If the effect that you obtained is big, you simply say that you have a big effect size! There are formal statistics used to estimate effect size and there are standard benchmarks that researchers use to comment on just how big an effect is, but generally speaking, effect size simply speaks to how big a statistical effect is.

In combination, information about statistical significance (if some effect found in a sample likely generalizes to a broader population) and effect size (how big a statistical effect is) provides us key insights about whether some finding in our research is a "big deal" and is "worth talking about."

# Use Computers to Help With Statistical Analyses

In a solid undergraduate psychology curriculum, you will usually have a component dedicated to learning the nuts and bolts of either Statistical Package for Social Sciences (SPSS) or R. These two statistical software packages are considered the cutting-edge packages to professionally compute statistics for the behavioral sciences. I personally use SPSS (as R came out after I completed graduate school).

One common way that the computer element is integrated into the curriculum is to have a special laboratory section associated with a statistics class that is partly dedicated to teaching about how to use the software to compute the kinds of statistics that you are learning in class. Thus, in class one day, you might learn how to compute a between-groups $t$ test (which allows you to see if means from two groups are significantly different from one another) and then the next day in lab, you might learn how to enter data into a spreadsheet so that it could be analyzed via a between-groups $t$ test. And then you might go ahead and use the computer software to conduct that test. The lab instructor (either the professor or, perhaps, a trained graduate student) would help walk you through the results and learn how to present them in a written and oral format.

# Demonstrate Psychology Information Literacy

Learning Outcome 2.2 from the *APA Guidelines* is all about demonstrating what we call *psychology information literacy*. A major part of this kind of literacy pertains to the ability to use a program like SPSS or R to compute analyses and knowing how to report the results from such analyses. This experience in your statistics class is all about developing this set of skills.

# Paths That Follow From a Solid Statistics Education

The topic of careers in psychology is addressed in detail in Chapter 11, but it seems appropriate to briefly comment here on the issue of statistics-related jobs. People are often surprised to see that a psychology major might set someone up for a career in statistics or scientific research, but it's true! The kind of rigorous statistics education that you will necessarily get in your undergraduate psychology curriculum will prepare you for all kinds of potential career paths.

Remember that we started this chapter by talking about how most people are scared of statistics. Well, once you have successfully aced this class, you will no longer be scared of stats. And you may end up like me, actually loving statistics!

Being good at stats is a truly important and rare skill out there in the work world. Statisticians are needed in the insurance industry, the field of educational research, higher education, business, health departments, and more. I have seen people with psychology backgrounds, in fact, get into strong careers in each of these areas based primarily on their statistical expertise. Even where SPSS and such tools are not used in the workplace, employers nonetheless view a job candidate's facility with statistics as a measure of his or her persistence and resilience. So yes, this is one more reason to take your statistics classes very seriously!

# The Bottom Line

Statistics is a foundational aspect of any psychology major. To study and document psychological phenomena in a useful manner, you need to understand statistics. Further, you need to be effective at presenting results of statistical analyses to others. Fortunately, statistical questions map onto all kinds of questions that we have about the world around us, making statistics a highly useful and relevant set of mathematical skills. Learning about the basics of statistics will allow you to thrive in your research projects in college and graduate school, and it will set you on an important potential path toward jobs in various research industries.

# Psychology Is a Real Science
## Part II. Research Methods in the Behavioral Sciences

7

efore we get into "why research methods?" in a detailed way, let's take a moment to step back and think about psychology as a science. The question of whether "psychology is a science" is actually a total nonquestion, although you will find people debating it here or there. A scientific field is one that is focused on predicting, understanding, and explaining some set of observable phenomena. This concept of *observable phenomena* simply refers to things that can be observed in the world. You can observe a ball bouncing on the street. You can observe a can of soda spraying wildly upon being opened after having been shaken. You can observe a dog make a playful gesture toward another dog at the park. These are all observable phenomena. Psychologists will often refer to observable phenomena as *empirical phenomena*; these are synonymous concepts.

Scientific disciplines, which often overlap with one another, can be defined in terms of the kinds of observable phenomena that they seek to understand, predict, and explain. Table 7.1 presents some examples that can help us understand different scientific fields in this manner.

Importantly, note that these different scientific fields correspond to basic (as opposed to applied) scientific areas. Most of these have various applied areas that are connected with them (e.g., engineering is an applied area that is connected with physics; social work is an applied area that is connected with sociology).

http://dx.doi.org/10.1037/0000127-007
*Own Your Psychology Major! A Guide to Student Success,* by G. Geher

**TABLE 7.1**

Sample Observable (i.e., Empirical) Phenomena and Basic Scientific Fields
to Which They Correspond

| Scientific field of inquiry | Kind of phenomena studied |
|---|---|
| Chemistry | Interactions among different basic physical elements |
| Biology | The living world (including physical qualities of organisms) |
| Physics | The world of physical objects |
| Geology | The physical earth |
| Astrophysics | The universe and its elements |
| Sociology | Outcomes connected with human social structures |
| Psychology | Behavior |

In this way, we can conceptualize psychology as the basic scientific area that is focused on understanding, predicting, and explaining behavior. In short, our field addresses the large-scale question: Why do people do what they do?

# What Are Research Methods All About?

In a broad sense, the science of psychology progresses by (a) developing theoretical frameworks (also known as *paradigms*), (b) asking questions that follow from these frameworks, (c) designing research to answer these questions, (d) examining the findings to determine the answers to these research questions, and then (e) informing the paradigm that was used guide the research in the first place. As such, research methods, which are traditionally featured centrally in a psychology curriculum, are part of a larger scientific process that is all about developing our best frameworks for understanding and making predictions about behavior.

The research methods portion of a psychology major is designed to map onto three learning outcomes from Goal 2 from the *APA Guidelines for the Undergraduate Psychology Major* (American Psychological Association [APA], 2013): Scientific Inquiry and Critical Thinking. These are as follows:

2.3 Engage in innovative and integrative thinking and problem-solving

2.4 Interpret, design, and conduct basic psychological research

2.5 Incorporate sociocultural factors in scientific inquiry

In addition, a research methods course also fulfills several outcomes from Goal 4: Communication:

4.1 Demonstrate effective writing for different purposes

4.2 Exhibit effective presentation skills for different purposes

4.3 Interact effectively with others

# The Tools of Research Methods

When I teach Research Methods, I like to make sure to put the entire idea of research methods into context. The tools that we use in our research methods are not ends in and of themselves. For instance, I will soon talk about ways to make sure that your study has something called *internal validity* (the degree to which you can be confident in saying that one variable in your study caused changes in another variable). Although internal validity and the other methodological concepts we have are important, we need to remember that they are tools: They are there to help us ask and answer questions about behavior.

Often, it is easy to get wrapped up in the details in all spheres of life. And, to be fair, at the end of the day, details are essential for absolutely everything we do. This said, as researchers, it is always important to remember *why* we are doing the research in the first place. If we are doing research, for instance, on an aspect of long-term memory, our goal is to better understand, predict, and explain long-term memory. We need to realize that our study itself is simply a tool in that bigger process of developing the best framework for understanding the phenomena that we are seeking to understand.

When a student is doing research in my class or in my lab, I am always asking the student questions such as, "How does this relate to the question that you are asking in the first place?" or "How can this methodology help inform the theoretical ideas that we are using to guide our research?"

As is true with the elements of statistics (and you know how much I love statistics!), all of the elements of the research methods that we use in psychology are simply tools designed to help us better understand behavior. My hope is that when you go into a class on research methods, you will make a point to always step back and see the details of the methods as not being ends unto themselves, but rather as tools that are designed to help us advance in our understanding of some aspect of behavior.

# Paradigms and Theoretical Concepts in Psychology

Research in psychology does not exist in a bubble. Research follows from our paradigms (or theoretical frameworks) that are designed partly as road maps to help guide research and partly as systems for understanding psychological phenomena. A *paradigm* is a set of interrelated concepts that essentially constitute a large-scale theory (or metatheory) designed to explain some phenomena.

In psychology, we have several instances of paradigms (see Kuhn, 1962), each with its own terminology, concepts, and assumptions. Some of the more significant paradigms in the field of psychology are found in Table 7.2.

As you can see, the paradigms in psychology vary considerably from one another. They vary in terms of their basic assumptions and key ideas. Therefore, you can bet

**TABLE 7.2**

Some of the Common Paradigms in Psychology

| Paradigm | Key concepts and assumptions |
|---|---|
| Behavior analysis | Mental concepts are not useful in psychology; we can understand behavior by understanding environmental factors such as primary and secondary stimuli in one's environment. |
| Feminist psychology | The field of psychology was created by men with substantial unconscious biases regarding how psychology works in humans. As women have become more empowered in the field, several key assumptions in psychology have been challenged. Psychologists need to always question the issue of gender in terms of the assumptions of research in the field of psychology. |
| Evolutionary psychology | The human mind is the product of thousands of generations of evolution, largely that took place before the advent of agriculture. Our minds and behavioral patterns are adapted, by natural selection and other evolutionary forces, for ancestral conditions from the African savanna. A key question to ask about any behavior pertains to how it helps to increase survival or reproduction. |
| Neuroscience | The mind is best understood in terms of its physiological substrates (e.g., the process of neural transmission). Behavior is a product of the nervous system. To best understand human behavior, we need to understand the physiological processes that underlie behavior. |
| Social constructionism | All psychological processes take place in social contexts. And social groups construct social realities—realities that may not be "real" in a physical sense but that are very real in a psychological sense that is shared among members of a community. It is this constructed reality that plays a primary role in shaping behavior. |

that the research that follows from these various paradigms will take on a certain form as a result of the particular paradigm that underlies it.

Suppose that a psychological researcher were going to study, for instance, aggressive behavior. You can see by the paradigms presented in Table 7.2 that the question being asked and the methodology being employed would vary considerably from one paradigm to the next. Examples of how research on aggression conducted by scholars who adopt these various paradigms might be as follows:

- A behavior analyst might carefully design a study to explore the degree to which a specific aggressive response in a child follows from the presence of a specific environmental stimulus (such as overly warm temperature in the testing room).
- A feminist psychologist might design a study to explore gender differences in reports of aggression in a sample of adults, predicting that males both engage in

more aggressive behavior and that they might encourage aggressive behavior in others at a higher rate as well.

▪ An evolutionary psychologist might design a study to explore the relationship between aggression in males and the presence of single females in the environment, predicting that male–male aggression evolved as a mechanism for securing mates.

▪ A neuroscientist might have a sample of participants agree to have their brains scanned using fMRI (functional magnetic resonance imaging) technology and examine which brain regions seem most active when the participants are asked to engage in aggressive thought activities.

▪ A social constructionist might study the social norms surrounding aggression that exist in two communities to see if different socially constructed norms lead to different levels of aggressive behaviors.

This set of five paradigms described here is only a sample of the paradigms that exist in psychology. As you can see, the paradigm that one uses as a starting point shapes the nature of the research one conducts in a profound way.

Just as students of research methods need to understand that the elements of our research methods are tools, and not ends in and of themselves, it is also important that students of these concepts realize how the basic assumptions, or paradigms, employed by a researcher will strongly drive the entire direction of a research program.

# The Empirical World and the Abstract (Theoretical) World

An important distinction in research methods is that between the empirical (observable) world and the abstract (conceptual, theoretical) world. *Theories, paradigms,* and *concepts* are all ideas. They are abstract. For instance, the feminist psychological conception of a masculinized culture that surrounds the field of psychology is an abstract concept.

On the other hand, empirical phenomena are just that: They are empirical, "real," and observable.

When we talk about the importance of testing a question to determine an answer, we will often say that we are dealing with *an empirical question* (in other words, we are saying that we need to ask if the phenomena in the world behave this way or that way). For instance, two psychology professors might be in a disagreement as to whether students who take a class in statistics early in their career do better in the program than do students who take this class later in their career. They might agree that as the answer is not yet known—that *it's an empirical question.* In other words, they are asking if the relevant phenomena in the world act a certain way and can be observed as such.

So let's get back to the conceptual idea of feminist psychology painting the field as being highly masculinized due to the historical origins of the field (being created mostly by men).

If we are going to research this question, then we would need to come up with some way to observe phenomena that would follow from this theoretical premise.

So the question then becomes this: How do we test this idea? Well, first we need to focus the question. The idea of psychological ideas simply being male biased based on the history of the field is too broad an idea to study empirically. So we need to break it down to something that can be observed. In fact, in a sense, the entire trick to doing research is to take a theoretical concept and convert it to a question that exists fully in the empirical world.

Shelly Taylor and her colleagues (2000) posed a question that challenged a primary assumption in the field of psychology, and the idea was rooted in the larger idea that a masculine worldview had shaped the field of psychology in a way that did not take the psychology of women sufficiently into account.

A long-standing concept in psychology pertains to what is called the *fight-or-flight response*, that is, the tendency for the body, when presented with a threatening stimulus, to mobilize either to get into a physical fight or to flee the situation. In fact, for decades, this idea has been essentially considered a truth in the field. Taylor and her colleagues (2000), coming from a feminist perspective, questioned whether the standard fight-or-flight response might be a typical male kind of response to a threat, but it may not be typical of females. In a review of several studies on female responses to threatening stimuli, these researchers, in fact, found that females regularly demonstrate what they refer to as a "tend and befriend" response to threats, becoming hyper-helpful, compassionate, and other-oriented in such conditions. This is, of course, very different from wanting to fight or flee! And this question really was only made possible by the assumptions of the feminist paradigm.

In any case, to the point at hand, research questions, such as whether males and females respond differently from one another when faced with threatening stimuli, need to be stated in testable ways. Theoretical ideas exist, by definition, in the abstract world—tests of these ideas exist in the empirical world.

# Asking Research Questions

Learning Outcome 2.3 from the *APA Guidelines* pertains to engaging in innovative and integrative thinking and problem solving. In fact, this is what the entire enterprise of research is all about. The process through which we ask research questions, which is a primary step in any research program, highlights this facet by focusing on the development of innovative questions and developing ways to test these questions that require much in the way of integrative thinking and problem-solving.

Research questions start in the abstract, theoretical world. The trick with a good research question is to carry the spirit of the abstract idea into your research. The more that your research question matches the theoretical question of interest, the more you are able to extrapolate your findings to the broader issues that you really care about.

The process of asking a research question includes the following steps:

1. framing the research question in an abstract and theoretical manner;
2. teasing apart the variables that are embedded in the question, staying in the world of theoretical ideas, for now; and
3. coming up with ways to *operationally define* each of your variables so that you can now move forward to actually testing the question.

An operational definition of a variable is an observable, empirical, quantifiable way to study that variable. So we can think of academic aptitude as a theoretical concept, and then we can think of one's Scholastic Aptitude Test (SAT) score as an operational definition of that concept.

Let's walk through these three steps in formulating a research question (or hypothesis) using an example.

*Step 1: Formulating the question at the theoretical level.* Suppose that a neuroscientist found that a particular class of nutrients increased serotonin activity in the brain and had reason to believe that because serotonin increases connectivity among neurons in the brain, students who regularly eat foods with these nutrients would score higher on measures of academic aptitude than those in a control group.

So here we have the research question framed in a theoretical manner: Do people who eat more fish show increases in serotonin activity and, as a result, score higher on measures of academic aptitude?

Well there is a straightforward research question, steeped in the fundamental framework of neuroscience. So far, so good.

*Step 2: Teasing apart the variables.* How many variables do we have in our proposed study? We've got three, actually. And remember, as we are still at Step 2, we are still in the abstract, theoretical world. The first variable pertains to how much of the special nutrient people take in. That varies among people, so this is a variable. The second variable pertains to the amount of serotonin in one's brain. Serotonin is a chemical that is released by brain cells (neurons) that has been shown to increase connections among neurons in general. Finally, our outcome variable is academic aptitude. So if we are going to conduct a study testing this model, we would need to come up with operational definitions of (a) intake of the special (hypothetical) nutrient, (b) serotonin activity, and (c) academic aptitude.

*Step 3: Operationally define your variables.* Now we need to operationally define each variable. Thus, we need to come up with a specific way to measure (or manipulate) each of these three variables. The amount of the nutrient taken in would probably be the kind of variable that we would operationally define by manipulating—creating different levels of this among different groups of participants. We could, for instance, have members of one group take 50 milligrams a day of the nutrient and then have members of another group take none. OK, we are getting somewhere. Next, we would need to measure serotonin activity in the brain. Wow, that doesn't seem easy! Here, we would need to use some brain activity measurement process designed for this purpose (and, as luck would have it, there is, in fact, equipment that does exactly this, such as the fMRI process we mentioned earlier). Finally, we would need to operationally define academic aptitude. We could administer the participants with a set of items from the SAT (assuming that our participants are old enough for that test).

Operationally defining your variables is an absolutely critical step in the research process. Once your variables are operationally defined, you can start to think about what data collection is going to look like. Importantly, always remember that your operational definition is a proxy for the conceptual variable that you are interested in studying at the theoretical level.

*Step 4: Restating your prediction using operational definitions.* Now that we have developed operational definitions for our variables, we can restate our hypothesis using these definitions. And once we have done this, we are ready to put the study together and start collecting data. In the current case, we would predict that participants who are randomly assigned to the high-nutrient-level condition would score higher than participants in the low-nutrient-level condition in both (a) serotonin levels and (b) the academic aptitude measure (created from a subset of SAT items).

# Two Basic Kinds of Methodologies

Learning Outcome 2.4 from the *APA Guidelines* focuses on interpreting, designing, and conducting basic psychological research. In fact, these goals are among the most central goals of a standard psychology curriculum. Your research methods class will be the core part of the curriculum where you begin to develop these skills.

There are many kinds of methodological designs out there. And any question framed at the theoretical level usually has a large number of methods that can be used to study it. There is an important lesson there: Because research questions start in the abstract, theoretical world, there truly are an infinite number of ways to test any research question. And there is never one right way to do it. Similarly, note that all of the variables in any study start out at the conceptual, abstract level and that they each can be operationally defined in an infinite number of ways. These ideas are important for students to understand because they encourage you to take a progressive approach to research. Don't let yourself get stuck because you are looking for the single best way to operationally define some variable—there is no such way! Any and all operational definitions of variables are simply proxies for the conceptual, abstract form of the variable.

While many techniques are used in psychological research, there are two basic kinds of methodologies: *correlational research* and *experimental research*. Correlational research is research that examines variables in their natural settings without altering them in any way, just measuring them as they exist. The point of a correlational study is to document the relationships among multiple variables. And this can come in a broad variety of ways.

Suppose you wanted to conduct a large-scale study of the relationship between diet and life satisfaction. Specifically, suppose you predicted that the more processed foods one eats, the less satisfied with life he or she is, and vice versa. To conduct this study, you might collect data on people's diets (perhaps via food diaries) and then have them complete an existing measure of life satisfaction. To be able to generalize your study to the broader population at hand, you might be very ambitious and try to collect data from more than 200 adults in each of the 50 states.

Now suppose that you did this study and ended up finding a relationship as you predicted: People who eat fewer processed foods are more satisfied with life than are others, and vice versa. Not bad—you'd have done well. In fact, because you studied real people, and lots of them, you could probably make the case that your findings demonstrate *external validity*, meaning that your findings likely generalize beyond your particular study. That's great.

However, you have conducted a correlational study, not an experimental study. So there is a liability with your study as well. Namely, you cannot make *causal inferences*—that is, you are not able to say that the kind of food that people eat causes their levels of life satisfaction. Because your study is correlational in scope, for reasons that you will learn about in detail in your research methods class, there are a number of reasons that your variables might be related—none of which may have to do with the effects of nutrition on life satisfaction directly! For instance, people who eat less processed food might be wealthier than their processed-food–eating counterparts, and although money can't buy love, it may have some positive effects on life satisfaction. And several other such *confounding* variables might exist as well. This is the downfall of correlational research.

But that's OK, we also have experimental research in psychology! An *experimental* design is one in which the variable that you think causes changes in the outcome is carefully manipulated by the researcher. So we could see the kind of food one eats as an *independent variable* (i.e., the variable that the researcher thinks is causing changes in the outcome). To do this, the researcher would need to randomly assign participants to be in one of two groups: A group that primarily eats nonprocessed foods and a group that eats primarily processed foods. The researcher would work carefully to make sure that the diets of the people in the two groups were highly controlled throughout the study period. Then the researcher would see, at the end of the study, whether the members of the two groups differed in terms of their mean scores on the dependent (or outcome) variable. In this case, the dependent variable would be scores on the life satisfaction measure (as with the correlational version of this study). Now suppose that you were able to get 100 people to be in each condition. And then you found that the participants in the nonprocessed-food condition scored higher on the life satisfaction scale. Good for you! Now, you have shown that these variables are related *and* that it is most likely the case that the kind of food that was eaten was causally related to the outcome. You can do this because you used a true experimental design, which allows you to make causal inferences because you have randomly assigned participants to conditions and have, as such, designed a study so that the only thing that differed across the two groups was the kind of food eaten during the study period.

In this second study, you can make the case that you have a high level of internal validity, which means you have confidence that the findings were due to a causal relationship between your variables.

Interestingly, internal validity and external validity sort of rub up against each other. The more internal validity you have, the less that your study takes place in the real world—and, thus, the less you are able to make inferences to the real world beyond your study (so you have less external validity). In a good correlational study, your data collection exists in the real world and, thus, you have high external validity. However, because you have not randomly assigned participants to different levels of the independent variable, your results are open to all kinds of interpretation and you are lagging in the domain of internal validity.

For the reasons spelled out here, note that it is often best to have multiple studies, including a combination of correlational and experimental studies, to provide comprehensive answers to our research questions.

# The Importance of Replication

In psychology research, we are studying human behavior, which is famously complex and is famously caused by a broad array of factors. As such, off the bat, we need to be skeptical of any research findings.

In a highly provocative set of papers (see Bonett, 2012), many well-accepted findings in the field of psychology were documented as being difficult or impossible to replicate. Think about that! Sometimes a finding from a study does not replicate because the original "finding" was spurious, meaning that the data happened to show a significant effect, but it was simply obtained by random chance. Further, many studies that are conducted in one location might end up totally failing to replicate in another location with a different cultural group. This particular fact demonstrates the importance of Learning Outcome 2.5 from the *APA Guidelines*, which focuses on the need to incorporate sociocultural factors in scientific inquiry.

So one lesson of the so-called replication crisis in the field pertains to the importance of studying phenomena across a broad range of cultural groups, especially if you are, as a researcher, trying to make inferences about human psychology in general. Further, this crisis reveals a simpler implication: We need to replicate our findings.

Suppose that you have conducted the two hypothetical studies described in the prior section: a correlational study and an experimental study on the relationship between diet and life satisfaction. Now suppose that in both studies, your hypotheses were supported. Should you stop there? Should science stop there? No, not at all! Given the complexities of human psychology, it is always a good idea to replicate a study's methodology and findings. If two correlational studies and two experimental studies provide the same pattern of findings, I become more convinced. And if three studies of each type replicate these same patterns, even better.

Replicating research might not seem very sexy, but it is a critical part of the scientific process. And because of the complex nature of human psychology, it may be more critical for our field than for just about any other.

# Additional Issues in Psychological Research

This chapter was designed to introduce you to some of the key concepts related to research methods in psychology and to put the entire idea of research in perspective, showing that the elements of our methodology are all tools to help us achieve greater theoretical understanding of behavior. As such, note that there is a lot more to research methods in our field than is presented here. Following is a brief delineation of some of the other basic concepts that you will be exposed to in your research methods education:

- *Complex designs:* Often, multiple variables are included in a study, including multiple independent variables, multiple dependent variables, and additional kinds of variables referred to as *covariates, mediator variables,* and *moderator variables,* which surround the relationships between independent and dependent variables.
- *Multiple forms of psychological measurement:* There are many ways to measure psychological variables, including performance tests, self-report, tests observations by others, measures of physiological stress responses, and more.
- *Ethical issues in research design and implementation:* Ethical issues show up at all levels of the research process, including the initial design of the study, the implementation of the study, and even the dissemination of findings. A broad array of ethical considerations is included in a standard research methods course.
- *Reliability and validity: Reliability* often refers to whether a measure in psychology is reliably measuring anything at all. *Validity* has various meanings in terms of research, ultimately speaking to the degree to which your findings and other elements of your study are legitimate.

# Developing Skills That Will Last a Lifetime

In my experience, Research Methods is often the course in the curriculum that students are most anxious about. It includes a lot of science and a lot of math—things that often scare off students. Further, it often includes a major research project that has all the elements of a full study, including conception, design, implementation, and presentation. As the famous Harvard psychologist, Robert Rosenthal was said to have quipped about this class: "Undergraduate students in a one-semester research methods class can only do an entire study in a single semester because they don't yet know that it's impossible to do so!" So yes, it is a lot! This said, there are really some great, transferable skills that you should walk away with from this class. These skills include

- the ability to formulate and test a research question;
- the ability to operationally define variables;
- the ability to choose the best study design to answer a particular question;

- the ability to write a strong research proposal;
- the ability to write a strong research report;
- the ability to present a research project orally;
- statistical software skills related to research;
- the ability to see how empirical research fits in with theoretical concepts;
- the ability to complete a major task by setting small, incremental goals; and
- three words: *time management, time management,* and *time management* (OK, that was way more than three words, but hey!).

To complement this list of skills, you'll also be practicing several communication skills, described briefly in the following sections. These are keyed to Learning Outcomes 4.1, 4.2, and 4.3 of *APA Guidelines* Goal 4: Communication.

## DEMONSTRATE EFFECTIVE WRITING FOR DIFFERENT PURPOSES

In your Research Methods class, you will most likely be writing quite a bit. And you will be likely completing assignments that have a broad array of functions, such as an *abstract*, which functions to provide a brief synopsis of a study for a broad audience, to a *research report*, which provides a detailed description of a study for an advanced audience.

Odds are that when you advance in any career, you will be asked to give reports. You may have a supervisor who asks you to write a report that summarizes earnings for a department. You might be a teacher writing a report regarding how well students in your class did on a recent standardized test. You might be a mental health counselor writing a report about how prevalent different anxiety disorders are in your practice. The skills that you obtain in writing a report for your research methods class will be transferrable to any of these situations.

## EXHIBIT EFFECTIVE PRESENTATION SKILLS FOR DIFFERENT PURPOSES

In a class in research methods, you will be presenting your work in a written format, but that's not all. Typically, this class includes an oral-presentation component where students learn to effectively present their work to others in a clear and coherent manner.

Just as you will likely be writing reports in whatever career path you end up in, you will likely be giving oral reports in some capacity as well. These may include big-time, formal reports, such as a report on a research study at an international conference in your field or simply summarizing some issue that has emerged in your work to a few coworkers in an effort to help fix some problem. In any case, you will be giving oral presentations in your work no matter what you end up doing. The oral-presentation skills that you obtain in the research methods component of your major will help set you up for success with such presentations.

## INTERACT EFFECTIVELY WITH OTHERS

Many of the assignments in a typical research methods class are group-oriented in nature. For instance, such a class will often have a separate weekly lab meeting in which students conduct group projects to learn some of the basic skills needed to conduct research (such as Statistical Package for Social Sciences labs on certain statistical processes). These group projects provide invaluable experience as group projects are a regular part of the real world waiting for you on the other side.

Research is usually a collaborative endeavor. And this is good preparation for so many things in life. In your work life, you can definitely expect to engage in all kinds of group projects. And you will find group projects emerging in work with community organizations and in managing a family. Life is full of group projects. The training that you get related to group projects in this class will be extremely useful for you as you advance on all fronts in life.

# The Bottom Line

OK, I'll admit it, not every student loves everything about research methods. This said, the content taught in this class is absolutely critical in the curriculum. The class allows a student an inside look into how ideas in psychology relates to the scientific process for generating ideas in the field. This class also provides students with a detailed and hands-on set of experiences related to all aspects of the research process in psychology. At the end of the day, a student who successfully completes this class should be well prepared for conducting advanced research in the field and making independent judgments on the quality of research conducted by others.

# ADVANCED RESEARCH AS A PSYCHOLOGY STUDENT | IV

One of the measures of student success as a psychology undergrad is whether you have a record of conducting research beyond your required coursework. Perhaps more so than any other discipline in the social sciences, scholarship in psychology incorporates students as true research collaborators. Chapters 8 and 9 are all about the nature of these kinds of opportunities, as well as the rich set of outcomes that follow from this kind of work as a student. Chapter 8 tracks along with the American Psychological Association's (APA's; 2013) *APA Guidelines for the Undergraduate Psychology Major* Goal 5: Professional Development, and Chapter 9 goes into detail on *APA Guidelines* Goal 4: Communication (which was introduced in Chapter 7).

## Chapter 8: Rolling Up Your Sleeves: Collaborating on Research Projects

Most psychology curricula include opportunities to do research with professors. This is often embedded in the curriculum, so that students can do this kind of thing for credit (as, for example, *independent study*). Students who take advantage of such opportunities often have a huge advantage in terms of getting into graduate programs and getting jobs after graduation. Further, the benefits that students gain from this kind of work are many. Students who conduct research with professors often get to travel to conferences (funded by the university), coauthor articles or chapters with professors, and more. These kinds of hands-on experiences are usually open to any student who knows how to look for them. This chapter provides guidance on that process.

## Chapter 9: Telling the World: Presenting Psychological Research Findings

In your psychology major, you will likely present psychological research findings in a variety of ways. For instance, you may be asked to write papers that summarize published research articles. Or you may give oral presentations that summarize published research articles. Further, you may have opportunities to present your own original research findings (such as research conducted as part of an independent study project) to a class. Or you may have the opportunity to present research (in oral or poster form) at a regional, national, or even international conference. The skills associated with presenting research are critical and highly transferable. This chapter describes how to find and take advantage of opportunities to present research and how doing this will benefit you as you develop professional skills.

# Rolling Up Your Sleeves
## Collaborating on Research Projects

8

T o this point, the conversation has focused on traditional classroom-based experiences within the psychology major. We talked about the importance of content-oriented classes (such as social psychology) and skill-oriented classes (such as statistics). But, remember from Chapter 2 where I said it's important to take an above-and-beyond approach to your education? And I made the case for truly owning your major? Well, here is where we really get into it: Students who take advantage of research collaboration opportunities are the ones who really shine. Let that be you—and watch all kinds of doors open to you as a result.

Although there are several kinds of above-and-beyond opportunities that a student might have available in his or her academic community, for my money, collaborative research with a professor's research team is really the ultimate above-and-beyond opportunity. This chapter describes the nature of these kinds of opportunities, addresses how they dovetail with Goal 5 of the American Psychological Association's (APA's; 2013) *APA Guidelines for the Undergraduate Psychology Major*: Professional Development, and provides several vivid examples of student research in action. It's my goal to inspire you to get involved in research and to provide you with clear examples so that you get a sense of the many ways you can get involved at this level.

http://dx.doi.org/10.1037/0000127-008
*Own Your Psychology Major! A Guide to Student Success*, by G. Geher

# What Does "Research With a Professor" Mean?

If you had asked me what a professor does in his or her job when I was a new freshman at the University of Connecticut in the late 1980s, I would have woefully missed the mark. Upon being asked this, at first I probably would have confessed to not having thought much about the question whatsoever.

I knew that professors taught; that was obvious. But I don't think I could have come up with much else that they did! And I don't think I had any clue as to how the duties of a professor differ markedly from the duties of a high school teacher.

I am writing this book so that you are better prepared for all of this than I was! Here's the deal: Professors have three broad areas of work expectations. These expectations include (a) *teaching*, (b) *scholarship*, and (c) *service*. Depending on the university and particular situation, a professor may teach only one class a semester, or four or five classes a semester. Four classes is considered a very heavy load, by the way. In addition to work as a teacher (which includes office hours so that students can access the professor outside the classroom), professors engage in scholarship.

Scholarship essentially has to do with knowledge production. This includes conducting research in one's area of specialty. So a neuroscientist might collect data on patterns of neural transmission. A social psychologist might collect data on the effects of situational manipulations on helping behavior. A developmental psychologist might collect data on how 2-year-olds differ from 4-year-olds in their responses to having their toys taken away. In addition to this "data collection" component of scholarship, professors need to produce in terms of scholarship. That is, it is not considered enough just to do research. A professor's research needs to lead to what we call *scholarly products*. This can take a few different forms, such as (a) giving presentations on the work at a national conference, such as the annual convention of the American Psychological Association; (b) publishing the findings in a book chapter edited by a different scholar in the field; (c) publishing the findings in a peer-reviewed journal as an article; or (d) writing a book that describes the research along with its implications. Professors who fail to produce a sufficient amount of high-quality scholarly products might be denied tenure (which is a polite way of talking about getting fired!). So scholarship is an important part of the job.

Finally, professors must engage in service as part of their job. Service means that a professor is contributing to the academic community (broadly defined) in various ways. At a local level, this might mean that the professor is on a committee in the department to help oversee the development of new classes, or a professor might be on a campus-wide task force to address an important issue such as gender, cultural, and intellectual diversity on campus. Service also extends beyond the campus. A professor might volunteer to review proposals for potential talks to be presented at a national conference. A professor might join the editorial board for a scholarly journal to help ensure that the articles being published in that journal are of high quality. A professor might take on an officer position with a scholarly organization (such as being president of the Association for Psychological Science). And so forth.

Relevant to the current conversation, the scholarship component of a professor's job is of particular importance. In some fields (such as history), professors tend to do their scholarly work all by their lonesome. A historian usually conducts his or her work independently. In some fields, scholarly work is usually done in a team-based manner. And this is how things are typically done in the field of psychology. The main reason for this is that scientific research projects in psychology are large and multifaceted, benefiting from various individuals taking on different roles.

In my work on research over the years, I have developed an approach to research that is very team oriented. We call our team the New Paltz Evolutionary Psychology Lab, and at any given point we will have about five undergraduates and five graduate students on the team. We meet once a week as a group (and there are always several smaller meetings throughout the week as well). And we always have between five and 10 research projects going on at any given time. As you can imagine, there is a lot that needs to be done—and we are deeply dependent on the students on our team to play a substantial role along the way!

The remainder of this chapter elaborates on the various ways that student research beyond the classroom can take place for students in the psychology major as well as the benefits that student receives from engaging in this kind of activity.

# Student Research as Professional Development

Many of the experiences built into the psychology major work toward Goal 5 from the *APA Guidelines for the Undergraduate Psychology Major*: Professional Development. Given the large focus that so many in the field place on research, joining a research team is definitely one great way to acquire skills related to the research-oriented professions in the field of psychology. Specific ways that this experience can help provide professional development are found in the following Learning Outcomes:

5.1 Apply psychological content and skills to career goals
5.2 Exhibit self-efficacy and self-regulation
5.3 Refine project-management skills
5.4 Enhance teamwork capacity
5.5 Develop meaningful professional direction

Many students majoring in psychology have career goals directly related to research in the field. Joining a research team as a student is perhaps the best way to acquire the skills in this area. Joining a research team is essentially the equivalent to doing a high-caliber internship in psychological research.

As mentioned earlier, psychological research usually takes the form of teamwork, with individuals being delegated specific modules of a larger project. This kind of experience helps develop self-efficacy (the belief that one can complete specific tasks; see Bandura, Barbaranelli, Caprara, & Pastorelli, 1996), along with self-regulation (the ability to monitor oneself to help work toward the team's research goals; see Baumeister & Vohs, 2004).

Perhaps no other part of the psychology curriculum is as project-based as is research that is done outside the classroom. Research is, at the end of the day, all project-based. When a student who signs up to join my team asks me about the time commitment, I usually laugh a little because the answer always is: It depends. When you are doing work that is project based and not time based, the goal is 100% about completing the project within a given timeframe and 0% about how much time is put into it. Developing project-based skills in this capacity is invaluable in teaching students, firsthand, the importance of getting things done over putting in such-and-such amount of time.

Given the importance of a project-based mind-set that is essential when it comes to research, a student and professor will need to work out a clear understanding regarding the workload and tasks that the student will be doing. And it's important that the student not take on too much. Many students these days have a full course load, a part-time job, responsibilities to a student organization or two, and so on. As such, organizing and managing time so as to be able to take on a collaborative research project is critical and it should be done in close coordination with the professor and the other team members.

Having a research project done in a team-based manner puts gentle pressure on each member of the team. In my research lab, I often delegate tasks for a project to five to seven students, with the goal of getting each task done before our meeting a week later. Trust me, students do not want to be the weak link in this process! No one wants to be the one to say, "Well, I didn't do my part, so this project cannot progress at this point." And this experience reflects what the real world is like. Joining a research team is an outstanding way to develop team-related skills.

Students who participate in a research team often develop a clear sense of their professional direction along the way. Some students connect strongly with the research process and, as a result, come to focus on research as a potential career path. Others focus on some of the content in the research that might relate to a career path that is not directly related to research. For instance, my research team is currently conducting a series of studies on the relationship between social estrangements and mental health. Several students on the team are interested in going into a career that relates to mental health, and this research is helping them get firsthand experience exploring issues in that area.

# Conducting Research With a Professor: Why? When? How?

As described in the earlier sections, there are several great reasons why a student should join a professor's research team. Such an experience helps build one's skills regarding teamwork, project management, and presenting information. Your future employers will certainly want to see teamwork skills on your resume, especially if you work in sales (as about 20% of bachelor's level psychology graduates do), professional services (17%), or management/supervision (16%; Stamm, Lin, & Christidis, 2016).

Research team experience might lead to such outcomes as presenting at scholarly conferences or even coauthoring a publication. Without question, all of these outcomes are to the benefit of the student—and these experiences are exactly what sets some students apart. And, for what it's worth: My advice is that if there are any opportunities that come your way where you can set yourself apart from the pack, run—don't walk!

To the question of when you want to join a professor's research team, there are lots of possibilities. I have seen the whole range on this one. For instance, I met my student Sara when she was a 17-year-old freshman at Western Oregon University. She was in my Introductory Psychology class, and wow, what a smart student she was! She seemed to understand everything immediately, and her papers for that class were written as if by a professional. At the end of the term, I asked her if she'd like to join my research team, and she agreed. She worked with me for the full year (before I left for another job in another state). She helped me design and collect data for two or three projects, leading, in fact, to at least one published book chapter with her name on it and one peer-reviewed article in a scholarly journal. I moved back east, but I always stayed in touch with Sara. She married Ben (who was also a student of mine) and they went on to have a family. One day, I had a book contract in-hand for a textbook on statistics. I needed a coauthor, someone who could take on many of the tasks, such as adding in graphs and tables, that I really didn't have the time for. I immediately thought of Sara—and she said yes. She is now the second author of *Straightforward Statistics: Understanding the Tools of Research* (Geher & Hall, 2014). And this all came out of her joining my research team her freshman year.

More typically, a student might join a research team at a more advanced stage, often around junior year or so. And there are some folks who argue that students who take on this experience should have successfully completed the course in research methods first. I do think there is some wisdom to this. But my broader point is that there is no single right time for a student to join a research team in a department. I usually tell students, as a rule of thumb, that if there is a professor who talks about his or her research and you find you connect with and are excited by that research, you should start a conversation about collaborating with that professor.

In terms of *how* you come to join a professor's research team, again, there are a few routes. Sometimes a professor might put out a call for research assistants. Or sometimes a student might come to have a good working relationship with a professor and then join the team as a result.

One thing that students should keep in mind: Joining a research team does not need to get in the way of your academic progress. There are typically several ways within the curriculum that a student can join a research team, including the following:

- *Signing up for a class* (often called *independent study*) designed for students to get credits toward the degree by taking on this kind of experience. Usually, students can sign up for this class for more than one semester.

- *Conducting an undergraduate thesis.* Undergraduate thesis options usually vary from department to department and school to school, but many schools and departments have this as an option, and the experience is a great way to collaborate with a professor.
- *Campus-wide research grants.* Many schools these days provide opportunities for students to conduct research with a professor either during the school year or during the summer. Often, these are paid experiences—not bad!

In terms of how to find out about these kinds of opportunities at your school, I suggest that you have a brief meeting with either your academic advisor or with the department chair; either of them should be able to point you toward the processes for making these kinds of experiences happen at your institution.

# What's Involved in Being a Part of a Research Team?

You might be wondering what all being in a research team entails. Let me start by saying that I am a bit biased: I think that overseeing my university's evolutionary psychology lab is pretty much the highest honor of my life and there is nothing I'd rather do than work with my students on research. The other day someone asked me if there were some semesters that I do not run the research team. Without hesitation, my answer was this: "I will run that lab until I am dead." And I truly believe this! So, again, I may be biased, but I think that the work involved in doing research is just awesome.

As I mentioned before, research is an incredibly project-based endeavor. And to get a project done, you simply have to do what all is needed to get the project done! That is to say that any particular project will have its own details and tasks. Some of the common tasks involved in psychological research include

- writing surveys or questionnaires;
- uploading surveys into online survey format;
- completing IRB (institutional review board) forms;
- collecting data from participants in a laboratory room;
- entering data into a spreadsheet;
- analyzing data using Statistical Package for Social Sciences (SPSS) or a similar statistical package;
- sending out a link to a survey to participants;
- writing part of a manuscript that summarizes a study, with an eye toward publication; and
- submitting a proposal to give a presentation on the research at a conference.

This all said, each and every study is unique and thus will have its own needs. To put a particular face to the experience, here I summarize a study from our lab that included generations of student collaborators. As you will see, the work was multifaceted to be sure!

# Case Study: The Neanderthal Project Revisited

If you have an open mind, you never exactly know where life is going to take you. For instance, the research from my research team on the personality of the ancient Neanderthals (described in some detail in Chapter 1) was never close to a project that I ever would have expected to be part of. But now, this work has been covered both in *Newsweek* and on National Public Radio (in the United States) and the *Guardian* (in the United Kingdom), along with several other media outlets around the world. In many ways, this ended up being one of the biggest and best research projects I've ever been fortunate to be part of. And, as is true with most of my research projects, it was a huge team effort that was successfully done in collaboration with several students.

In 2014, a biological anthropologist from New York University, Todd Disotell, came to our campus to speak in a speaker series that I oversee called the Evolutionary Studies (EvoS) Seminar Series. Professor Disotell's talk was on the topic of Neanderthal–*Homo sapien* hybridization. Yes, that means what you think it means! As a researcher who uses molecular DNA analysis in his work, he was one of the scholars who provided evidence that, going back about 40,000 years ago, there were some "hybridization events" between ancestrally modern humans and Neanderthals. Further, as if that is not spectacular enough to think about, get this: Many of us alive today have DNA markers that show strong signs of our being descended from these events. In other words, many of us have Neanderthal DNA in all the cells of our bodies!

Professor Disotell went on to discuss how modern personal genome companies, such as 23AndMe, actually provide each client with a statistic speaking to how much Neanderthal overlap he or she has, with the range typically being from about 0% to about 4%. So along with my colleague Alice Andrews, my students and I started to brainstorm. What if we could find a sample of people who completed 23AndMe and asked them to report their Neanderthal overlap (which we eventually came to call NQ for *Neanderthal Quotient*)? We could give these people a large battery of personality tests and then potentially draw conclusions about the Neanderthal personality based on which personality traits tend to be significantly associated with NQ.

So this idea got us pretty excited. The next day in the lab, we sat down and started the process of mapping out this idea. And there was plenty of work to be done to make this happen. The following are some of the specific tasks:

- Briana: Communicated with 23AndMe to see if they would be interested in collaborating on this project
- Gloria: Conducted an intensive literature review on the known features of the personality and social structures of the ancient Neanderthals to help guide our inclusion of certain trait measures
- Jess: Started the online survey via Qualtrics software
- Dave: Helped develop a system for coding open-ended responses designed to measure creativity

- Morgan: Played a lead role in organizing the SPSS data files and working with the other students to create subscales of our measures
- Scooter: Cleaned the data file and conducted several preliminary analyses
- Rich: Conducted basic statistical analyses, wrote the Method section, and wrote part of the Results section
- Vania: Played an important role in organizing the statistical analyses and organizing the structure of the final manuscript

Of course, I pitched in too, largely organizing and writing the bulk of the draft and submitting the paper for review at two journals. At first, we submitted it to an elite journal, *Science*. Given how competitive it is to get published in that journal, we were not surprised to have the paper rejected there. But I then submitted the paper to *Human Ethology Bulletin*, and although the editor had plenty of suggestions for revision and clarification, the bottom line was that they accepted and published it! This was, without question, a team effort—on a topic that I never would have thought I'd have studied in my career.

And, of course, the students who participated played invaluable roles in getting this work done and they now have a scholarly publication to their record as a result! On top of that, those students have ended up doing pretty well: Five of those students are currently enrolled in doctoral programs!

So, here we have several benefits that came out of the student collaborative work on this project. First, we advanced knowledge: Our work is cited as research that sheds light on the personality features of the ancient Neanderthals. Second, this work received media attention beyond the original scientific publication. So the ideas and findings found therein are now having an influence beyond just academia. Regular people out in the world are talking about them! Third, the students got great experience leading to a coauthored scholarly publication, which, of course, is the kind of thing that just looks great on a resume.

However, on top of all this, I'd be remiss if I didn't discuss one final benefit to collaborative research projects such as this one: It was a ton of fun! From the original brainstorming meeting to the day that we got the letter saying it was accepted for publication, this research was just a blast. It took a ton of time and energy, but I think that everyone involved would agree that it was worth it.

## The Bottom Line

Perhaps the single best way for a psychology student to get deeply involved is to join a research team. Most schools have various mechanisms for getting students involved as research collaborators with professors, and most psychology professors are thrilled to have students join them on their research journeys. Benefits of joining a faculty member in research are many. Ultimately, joining a research team may well be the single best way of setting a student apart from the rest of the pack. On top of that, as I hope I have explicated throughout this chapter: Collaborative research on a topic that you find interesting is nothing short of a blast!

# Telling the World
## *Presenting Psychological Research Findings*

9

oal 4 of the American Psychological Association's (APA's; 2013) *APA Guidelines for the Undergraduate Psychology Major* is all about communication. We got an introduction to the Communication learning outcomes in Chapter 7; for your convenience, here they are again:

4.1 Demonstrate effective writing for different purposes
4.2 Exhibit effective presentation skills for different purposes
4.3 Interact effectively with others

APA is right to place such a high premium on communication. As I tell my students, knowing information in a vacuum, without being able to effectively present it to others, is essentially useless. Sometimes a student will say something like, "Well, I totally understand the content, I just wasn't able to get that across in my essay, that's all." My answer to this: *No, this will not do—and sorry-not-sorry!* Knowing the information isn't even half the battle in my mind. Being able to effectively communicate ideas that you learn is absolutely essential.

As an example: Imagine you get your first job out of college. You have done well, and you landed a job on Madison Avenue at a major advertising firm. You are leading a team that put together a new plan to advertise for a major restaurant chain. You are slated to present the advertising plan to

http://dx.doi.org/10.1037/0000127-009
*Own Your Psychology Major! A Guide to Student Success*, by G. Geher

the board of directors of that business. You fumble, get a few words out, forget what your point was, and, well, the presentation ends up being a total flop. Don't worry, you are young yet, and life will have plenty of upcoming opportunities for you. This said, imagine if you e-mail the director of the board the next day and say something like, "I know that presentation wasn't all that great, but trust me, I really know what I meant to say." I don't know about you, but I personally wouldn't hold my breath waiting for a response!

Or imagine this: You recently completed your bachelor's degree in psychology with a concentration in applied behavior analysis, and you are were recently hired to work at a center for children who are on the autism spectrum. You completed an internship there while you were getting your degree, and they liked you enough to hire you full time. At some point, your supervisor asks you to give a brief presentation on the nuts and bolts of the work for a new group of interns. You neglected to put together any materials or to think much about the presentation, and you suddenly find yourself standing at the front of a room with 15 college students looking to you for some wisdom. You sweat and stutter for about 20 minutes—and the whole time you are thinking that you really should have prepared something! Later, your supervisor tells you that it's OK, but that you should think about preparing better next time.

Communication of ideas is essential. No matter what career path you end up following, you will absolutely need highly effective communication skills. If you are a researcher, you will need to be able to write summaries of your research for others to understand. If you are a school psychologist, you will have write and give oral reports on the issues of particular children in the district that you are working with. If you are an industrial–organizational psychologist, you will need to give presentations on plans you have for improving any particular workplace. And so forth. Communication is a foundational part of any career that follows from a psychology major. For this reason, APA places a strong premium on cultivating communication within the psychology major.

## Methods of Presentation

Within the psychology curriculum, presenting research is the primary way to develop your communication skills. Research presentations within the major come in a variety of written and oral formats. By the end of your undergraduate years, you should be able to give a brief synopsis of a research project, and a more elaborate summary. You'll be able to talk about a complex research idea to someone with a doctorate. And, as I tell my students, you should also be able to summarize a complex research idea for my mom in Florida—that is, in an interesting, jargon-free way.

Your undergraduate psychology curriculum will likely have various assignments and opportunities for you to develop your communication skills. And don't ever forget this: The more communication-based assignments that your professors give to you, the more they are trying to help you develop your communication skills to help set you up for success for the future.

With this said, note that developing communication skills is not always easy, and it often benefits from guidance. Your professors all have office hours, and they should all be reasonably expert when it comes to written and oral communication. My advice to you, then, is to seek out your professor for help with presentation-based assignments. Whether it is a paper or an oral presentation, meeting with the professor ahead of time should, without question, help you hone your thoughts on both the content and on the process by which you are trying to communicate the content. And never forget that helping you develop your skills is the primary job of your professor—it is why he or she gets paid. So don't be afraid to go and ask for help!

Following are some of the assignments and opportunities that you should expect to encounter within the major.

# Lab Reports

Depending on your particular program, you may have a number of classes that include lab components. These classes might include Introductory Psychology, Statistics, and Research Methods, among others. The point of a lab section is to get students to do some kind of practical, hands-on experience (such as collecting data from everyone in the class on some personality trait) and then presenting the small project in some coherent manner. A common assignment in this kind of class would be a brief written summary of the in-class project. An oral presentation of the project, including the methods and the findings, might be included as well.

# Extended Research Reports

You will likely have to produce at least one extended research project during your time in the major. This experience usually takes place in the Research Methods class, with a typical assignment including the design and implementation of an entire empirical project, including a 10- to 20-page written report of the project (often written with multiple drafts and lots of feedback from your professor).

# Extended Literature Reviews

You also will likely have at least one class (often a class called Advanced Seminar or something like that) in which you will need to write what we call an extended literature review. This is where you will read published articles, books, and book chapters on some focused area of psychological research, and then you will summarize the findings into a coherent, linear paper. Students often find this assignment challenging at first, and it benefits from meeting with the professor and getting extensive feedback. It is also the kind of assignment that builds great skills that connect the integration of ideas with communication.

# Abstracts

Sometimes you may be asked to write an abstract, or a brief summary of a study. One assignment I give is constrained to two pages, for instance. In that space, students need to describe an entire research project that they are proposing. This is a challenge! But it is great to get students to think about how to get their ideas boiled down into a succinct product. Trust me, this skill will benefit you long into the future.

# Oral and Poster Presentations

Being able to give an oral presentation on some set of ideas is essential. Effective oral communication skills will bring you far. In several classes in the curriculum, you are likely to have required oral presentations. You should see each and every such experience as an opportunity to develop yourself. Oral presentations on research will often be accompanied by slides in PowerPoint or something similar. I usually tell my students that they should have slides representing the introduction of the idea, the hypotheses, the methods, the results, and the conclusions. And usually the rule of thumb of one slide per minute works pretty well.

Another very common way to present research in psychology is via a poster presentation. A poster presentation is one in which you sketch out your ideas in text and images on a poster that is usually about 30 by 40 inches or so. Typically, this is done via PowerPoint or a similar kind of software. A good research poster presentation will often mirror the slides for an oral presentation, including sections for the introduction, hypotheses, methods, results, and conclusions. A poster presentation is usually given in a session, alongside several other presenters and posters. In this context, the audience comes around to many of the posters, and the presenters will give brief ("elevator" versions) of their research summaries. An elevator version of your presentation is pretty much a 2-minute summary (with the idea being that you are in an elevator with someone and have until that person gets off the elevator to get all of your points across).

# Presenting Ideas Beyond the Classroom

As you advance in your work as a budding behavioral scientist, you may find other kinds of opportunities to disseminate your ideas. Professionals in the field will often be called upon to write blogs, participate in podcasts, and take part in interviews with various forms of media sources, among other responsibilities. For instance, you might one day emerge as an administrator at a center that focuses on people with anxiety disorders. A journalist with a local newspaper may be writing a story about rates of anxiety in the United States today and may call or e-mail you to get your thoughts on the topic (as an expert in the field). As you will see, skills you develop during college related to presenting information will be extremely useful for your future.

# Presentation Venues

During your time as a psychology major, you will certainly be presenting ideas in the classroom. This will include giving oral presentations in class and producing written work. In fact, if you seek out extracurricular opportunities, you may well find additional venues for the presentation of your work. Additional venues may exist to present research in both written and oral formats. And yes, you should seek these opportunities out and take advantage of them.

# Venues for Written Work

Several venues exist for high-quality written work by psychology undergraduates. For a comprehensive list of these outlets, you should check out the website for the Council of Undergraduate Research. Some of the several journals dedicated to publishing high-quality undergraduate research include the following:

- *Undergraduate Journal of Psychology*
- *The Undergraduate Research Journal of Psychology at UCLA*
- *Journal of European Psychology Students*
- *Journal of Psychology and Behavioral Sciences*
- *EvoS Journal: The Journal of the Evolutionary Studies Consortium*

# On-Campus Conference Presentations

During your time in the major, you might have an opportunity to present research at one or more on-campus conference-like venues. Many schools have an entire day, usually in late spring, dedicated to such an event. At the State University of New York (SUNY) New Paltz, we have a day we call Minds at Work, which includes the Student Research Symposium (a large poster session including student researchers from across campus) among several other outlets for the presentation of student research and creative works. You should ask your advisor about such opportunities on your campus. And if no such opportunities exist, see about helping create such an event.

# Regional Conference Presentations

Students who are involved in research might have an opportunity to present their research at a regional psychology conference. Sometimes such a conference might be very small and local, such as the Mid-Hudson Psychology Conference that was held for a few years and that included student presenters from about five or six schools in the Hudson Valley. Beyond this, students are typically highly encouraged to attend meetings of broader organizations, such as Eastern Psychological Association or

Western Psychological Association. Such regional conferences are often considered very student-friendly, and presentations are given by a combination of students and professors.

In my own experience, I spearheaded the creation of the NorthEastern Evolutionary Psychology Society in 2007, a regional intellectual society dedicated to advancing research in the field of evolutionary psychology. As discussed in an special case-study section later in the chapter, you will see that many students over the years have reaped benefits from participating in this conference in various ways.

Conference presentations usually come in a few varieties, including an oral presentation (typically 15–20 minutes) or a poster in a poster session. Student presenters at such a conference have an extraordinary opportunity to meet students and professors with shared intellectual interests from other schools. These conferences are often great for networking and for learning about opportunities that exist beyond one's own campus.

# National and International Conferences

Sometimes students have the opportunity to present at larger conferences, including national and international conferences. Importantly, schools often have funding opportunities to help students with this kind of travel, especially if the students are going to present. So don't let the cost discourage you; ask your advisor about funding opportunities.

In the United States, the two biggest general psychology conferences are the annual meeting of the APA and of the Association for Psychological Science (APS). These conferences include all kinds of psychological researchers, with APA focusing more on applied, clinical areas of psychology and APS focusing more on basic research.

You will see that there are all kinds of specialized intellectual societies related to psychology as well, and often professors might choose to go to the meetings of these societies because they are more likely to have shared interests and connections with scholars at more specialized conferences. In any case, if the professor with whom you are doing research is planning to attend one of these conferences, speak up and get yourself to join. Attending off-campus conferences tends to be among the most inspiring and influential kind of experiences that a student might have in his or her academic career.

# Nonacademic Venues

Several nonacademic venues exist as well. Academic content is of interest to a variety of audiences and, therefore, you might find yourself presenting research to audiences that you had never even thought of. Such venues might include a local chapter of an organization such as the Rotary, a meeting of a local political action group, or a local business with an interest in some facet of your research, for example.

As an example, in February 2017, my research lab was invited by a group called the Hudson Valley Humanists to give a symposium (a set of brief presentations) on our research as part of the group's celebration of Darwin's birthday (it's a Humanist thing!). Six of my students agreed to take part. They each gave 10-minute presentations on their own particular research. The audience, a group of highly educated and friendly humanists, were extremely responsive, showing a deep and genuine appreciation for the work of my students. This was definitely the kind of research presentation that my students never would have thought they would be involved in when they first signed up to join our program.

A great thing about presenting research to a nonacademic audience is that you really need to develop the ability to unpack your ideas in a way that can be understood by someone outside your field. For this reason, I strongly encourage students to seek out opportunities to present their research ideas to people outside of their formal academic circle. You will see that it helps you see the relevance of your own work.

# The NorthEastern Evolutionary Psychology Society: A Case Study

Here's another case study, one regarding an intellectual society that, along with several of my students, I spearheaded in 2007.

When I started out my career in the psychology department at SUNY New Paltz, I came to find that my students and I seemed to like the field of evolutionary psychology much more than anyone else did! As a result, we decided to start our own society—one that would reach beyond the bounds of our own campus. We called it the NorthEastern Evolutionary Psychology Society (NEEPS) and designed it to be a student-friendly organization that would provide a forum for students from all across the region to present on their research via both oral and poster presentations.

The first conference, held on our home campus in 2007, was a bigger hit than we had expected. Not only did professors and students from all over the Northeast come, but people came from several provinces in Canada, as well as from California and the United Kingdom. Student participation has been a hallmark of NEEPS, and you probably know me well enough by now to know that I would not have it any other way! Some of the student-related highlights of NEEPS over the years are as follows:

- Student volunteers regularly help host and organize the program for the annual conference.
- Students play a major role in some of the "fun" activities of the conference such as the designing of the annual T-shirt.
- Students regularly give both poster and oral presentations at the conference.
- Awards are given each year to students for outstanding poster and oral presentations.
- All presenters, including students, are encouraged to submit papers based on their findings to our two affiliated journals: *Evolutionary Behavioral Sciences* and *EvoS Journal: The Journal of the Evolutionary Studies Consortium*.

- Students get to network with professors and students from other schools, often forming important working relationships, including research collaborations.
- Partly via networking, students at NEEPS often find their ways into graduate programs of professors at other schools based on having met them at NEEPS.

and more!

As we can see from the example of NEEPS, conferences and their parent intellectual societies provide tremendous opportunities for student researchers in psychology. Although there are clearly many pieces of advice that any professor can give to any student, based on my experiences in working with psychology students over the years, I would definitely say that presenting research at a conference, and participating fully in the conference proceedings may be the single best way to get the most out of your psychology education.

# The Bottom Line

Given all of the successes I have seen from student researchers in my career, I cannot understate the positive impact of engaging in research as a student. The benefits are multifaceted and often exceptional.

Presenting research is, in a sense, a necessary culmination of the work that has been done. Although there are many aspects to the research experience, if the work is not presented in a cogent and accessible way to an interested audience, then it is unclear if the research was worth doing in the first place. Your institution's psychology curriculum will include many kinds of opportunities for students to present on their research in both written and oral formats. Further, professors in most psychology programs can help students present their research at conferences, on campus and off, leading to a host of opportunities. There are many great extracurricular experiences available to the psychology major but presenting one's research at a conference is hard to beat.

# PROFESSIONAL DEVELOPMENT: INTERNSHIPS, GRADUATE PROGRAMS, AND CAREERS

# V

R ooted in the curricular goals proposed by the American Psychological Association (APA), this book is designed to both inspire and guide undergraduate psychology students as they navigate the waters of their major in psychology. I hope you've felt both inspired and guided thus far! This final section focuses on the future and on how you can fully optimize your experiences in the major as you gear up for graduate study and/or for careers in the field. Chapters 10 and 11 relate to Goal 5 in the 2013 *APA Guidelines for the Undergraduate Psychology Major*: Professional Development, the learning outcomes of which were presented first in Chapter 8. Chapter 12 sums it all up for you.

## Chapter 10: How to Land (and Get the Most Out of) an Internship

Most psychology curricula include internship opportunities (such as in a class titled *Internship* or *Practicum*). Students with any interest in applied psychology (such as students who may want to do therapy or counseling as a career) should most definitely take advantage of such internship opportunities. Internship opportunities can take a variety of forms, including paid internships, credit-bearing internships, volunteer internships, and so forth. This chapter describes the various kind of internship opportunities that are typically offered to students, along with guidance on how to make the most of such opportunities.

# Chapter 11: Thinking About Careers and Graduate School

Psychology students have a broad array of graduate programs to which they might be interested in applying. Such programs might be master's or doctoral level. They might focus on applied psychology (such as a master's in mental health counseling), or they might focus on research (such as a doctorate in neuroscience). It turns out that there are many kinds of graduate programs related to psychology. Beyond graduate or professional coursework, there are various career paths that psychology majors are typically prepared to pursue. Psychology students end up in a variety of careers. These range from being researchers, professors, lawyers, doctors, occupational therapists, human resource specialists, applied behavior analysts, counselors, clinical psychologists, and more. The career options for psychology majors in this day and age are wide open. This chapter demarcates the various kinds of graduate programs that exist, along with the career trajectories that psychology students typically follow; it also offers structured guidance on how to reach your goals.

# Chapter 12: Cheat Sheet for Owning Your Psychology Major

The guidance provided in this book is multifaceted, touching on such varied aspects of your academic career as (a) the rationale for taking a course in statistics seriously, (b) how to see the psychology major as a way to develop a community-oriented approach to life, and (c) various venues for presenting psychological research. Clearly, there is a lot going on here! Consistent with the theme of cultivating student success, this final chapter puts it all together and provides, in good old top-10 list format, some bottom-line guidance for you as an undergraduate psychology student.

# How to Land (and Get the Most Out of) an Internship

10

oal 5 of the of the American Psychological Association's (APA's; 2013) *APA Guidelines for the Undergraduate Psychology* guidelines focuses on professional development. We got an introduction to the Professional Development Learning Outcomes in Chapter 8; for your convenience, here they are again:

5.1  Apply psychological content and skills to career goals
5.2  Exhibit self-efficacy and self-regulation
5.3  Refine project-management skills
5.4  Enhance teamwork capacity
5.5  Develop meaningful professional direction

In other words, your psychology major should prepare you for what lies ahead. As such, you can expect your program to have some form of internship opportunity embedded within the curriculum itself. This chapter focuses on internships, discussing such topics as (a) what the internship experience is all about, (b) how to obtain an internship, and (c) the many benefits that follow from a successful internship experience.

http://dx.doi.org/10.1037/0000127-010
*Own Your Psychology Major! A Guide to Student Success,* by G. Geher

# The Undergraduate Internship Experience

An internship (or *practicum*) experience is essentially a hands-on experience in which a student works in a professional setting, shadowing professionals in the field and often helping out with various tasks on an as-needed basis. Psychology students who have aspirations to work in the field of mental health will often participate in internships under the supervision of such professionals as clinical psychologists, school psychologists, school counselors, or mental health counselors.

A solid psychology curriculum will often have at least one internship experience embedded into the curriculum itself. That is, there is usually at least one course that a student can take that provides credit within the major for students. This class may be titled Internship in Psychology, or Practicum in Psychology, or the like.

An internship class typically includes two basic components: (a) an *in-class* component and (b) a *site* component. In such a class, the in-class component is usually taught by a professor who has strong applied experience him or herself. This may be a professor with a doctorate in clinical psychology and a long history of conducting psychotherapy, for instance. The class, which is often capped at a small number (e.g., 20) so that there is ample opportunity for discussion and participation, will usually include students who are working with a variety of placements. So a class of 20 or so students might be connected with five to 15 *placement sites* (i.e., locations where the students are actually working with a professional during other times in the week). During the class component of the course, time is dedicated to a combination of standard lecturing, with the professor discussing issues regarding work in the applied areas of psychology, along with time dedicated to discussion, when students can talk about some of the particulars of their placement with the group. The class will also include a number of readings and assignments designed to enhance the student's internship experience. A typical assignment for this kind of class would be the keeping of a journal that connects with the work that the student is doing on the site.

The placement component of the class is what makes it special. Typically, on the basis of prior agreements between the department and some local agencies, students will be placed in one of several possible locations working under the supervision of an experienced professional in the field. These placement sites will vary from one another in terms of the kinds of issues they address. Partly for this reason, it is typical for students to be able to complete the internship class more than once. This feature of the curriculum allows students either (a) to try an internship regarding a different population or area of applied psychology or (b) to advance and focus on the work at a site that is an extremely good fit for a student.

As already mentioned, placement sites might include a number of specialties, including placements such as working

- with a local clinical psychologist who is in private practice,
- with a local mental health counselor who is in private practice,

- with a local licensed clinical social worker who is in private practice,
- with a school psychologist in a local school district,
- with a school counselor in a local school district,
- at an agency that focuses on children with special cognitive needs,
- at an agency that focuses on children with special emotional needs,
- at an agency that focuses on adults with special cognitive needs,
- at an agency that focuses on adults with special emotional needs,
- at an agency that supports adolescents in an after-school program,
- at an agency that supports individuals and families that are struggling economically,
- at an agency that supports women and families, or
- at an agency that focuses on drug rehabilitation.

In fact, this list is not complete. On the basis of my experience working with students who have participated in internship experiences, I can tell you that there truly are many different areas available for students interested in internship experiences related to psychology.

Because the internship class is a *special* class within the curriculum, getting into it typically requires a bit of initiative. If you are a student in a program that has an internship class on the books but you have no idea how to sign up for it (yes, I've seen this scenario!), then you should meet with your advisor or with the chair of the department and ask about the process. The process for getting into an internship class typically includes scheduling an interview with the professor who will instruct the class. This interview is largely designed to see whether a student seems like a good fit for the experience. Seeming like a good fit often comes down to whether a student seems to have a good idea of what the experience is about and can talk about it in a professional manner. Reading this chapter will surely put any student a step ahead on this front.

Getting into the class is often not exclusively the result of the interview. Because these classes are usually capped to maintain low enrollment numbers, sometimes a student who interviews well will not be admitted to the class simply because of enrollment constraints. But this said, if the department has its ducks in a row and you interview early in the process and do well, you should be in good shape.

A next step relates to the placement process. Once you are authorized to take the class, you need to be placed with an appropriate agency under the supervision of an approved site supervisor. Usually, the internship professor will have a list of previously approved agencies that a student would be able to choose based on his or her interests. Sometimes, a student comes into the situation with a plan for a site. This often comes in the form of a family friend or someone else that the student knows already. These kinds of requests need to be dealt with by the professor on an ad hoc basis, examining each case separately and carefully. If you are reading between the lines, I am essentially saying that although these situations sometimes work out, it is often the case that the professor would prefer that an internship is conducted with one of the previously approved agencies, for a number of reasons.

For instance, working with an approved and department-affiliated agency includes institutional assurances that the supervisor is appropriately credentialed and that the nature of the work is appropriate. You don't want fetching coffee to be your sole activity as an intern—although, granted, that is an unlikely scenario. Although an internship with a family friend may well fit program criteria, it is usually the case that placement sites that have been vetted by the university and the department are most likely to provide a solid educational and developmental experience for students. (This said, as with much advice, this is really more of a guideline or rule of thumb rather than a hard-and-fast rule.)

The site-placement component of the work includes a certain number of required hours on site. The particular number will depend on the rules of the particular academic institution. At State University of New York (SUNY) New Paltz, the rule is that for a three-credit internship class, there is a requirement of 8 on-site hours a week. The details of the scheduling of the hours are usually worked out between the student and the site supervisor. This is an important point because students often worry that the scheduled hours for an internship will not be compatible with their schedule. Although this can be challenging, note that site supervisors are generally aware of scheduling issues and are collaborative in their approach to working with students to make sure things work out.

The work that is conducted in the internship setting can vary wildly. One thing is certain: This work will not include conducting therapy directly with clients. This point, often disappointing for students, is actually quite standard. In the fields related to psychotherapy and counseling, only those with the appropriate advanced degrees and license are typically able to actually conduct therapy and counseling. Nonetheless, depending on their particular stage, interns are able to help with all kinds of aspects of the work that surround the therapeutic processes, which might include such tasks as

- helping develop and implement programs for the agency;
- helping update and develop the web and social media presence of the agency;
- helping the clients with nonclinical aspects of the work, including details of scheduling and logistics; and
- working with individuals in a group setting that is not framed as therapeutic in nature (e.g., mentoring adolescents at an after-school program).

The internship experience described in this section focuses on the traditional kind of experience that a student would get within the confines of a standard undergraduate psychology curriculum. Importantly, note that, depending on one's interest, a psychology student may find himself or herself in an internship in any number of industries. Typical psychology internships may exist in a human resources office for a large company, the counseling department of a middle school or high school, the social work department of a local health care agency, or an advertising agency, for example. So when you are thinking about landing an internship, go ahead and work to match the internship with your particular interest areas within the field of psychology.

# Routes to an Internship Experience

Taking the class titled Internship or Practicum in the major, as described in the previous section, is a standard route to obtaining an internship experience within the undergraduate psychology curriculum—and it usually works well! This said, there are a number of alternative paths that the internship experience that students should be aware of.

# Summer Internships

College students often go home for the summer. They typically need to work. Concurrently, they usually would like to work in their field of study, if possible. As such, students are often looking for summer internship opportunities—opportunities that may not be directly affiliated with their school. In fact, I have seen this kind of thing work out in a number of ways. Sometimes a student may get lucky and find a paid summer internship opportunity back home, which is a good thing. Often a student in a situation like this will reach out to his or her advisor or department chair and ask if it is possible also to receive credits toward the major for this experience. Such as request can be a little tricky. Some schools have strict rules about this issue, insisting that a for-credit internship experience must not be a paid internship experience. Another issue to keep in mind pertains to the logistics. The department may not have the ability to offer a piecemeal internship class to a student over the summer. This said, these kinds of things are always worth asking about, and departments often do have systems for helping students make the most out of summer internship experiences.

# Specialized Internship Experiences in the Major

As elaborated in the next section, which summarizes a case study of a particular specialized internship program in Oregon, based on the particular interests and areas of expertise of the faculty in a department, there may be specialized kinds of internship experiences that are available to students in a particular department. For instance, at my university, we have a specialized undergraduate minor in disaster studies, a program that is run out of the psychology department. This minor includes a focused internship class, designed for students to conduct an internship with an agency that focuses on some element of disaster preparedness. For instance, many of our students complete internships with the Orange County Office of Emergency Management. This internship experience parallels the standard internship experience, described in the previous section, but it is a separate class with a separate kind of focus.

Another kind of specialized kind of internship might connect with the school's counseling center. A college or university will typically have a counseling center dedicated to helping college students with various mental health issues. As is true of any agency in this area, the individuals running the counseling center often could use the assistance of interns. In my department, we have a specialized internship class, separate from the other two that I have already mentioned, called *crisis intervention*. This class, which is usually taken across two or more consecutive semesters, has students help out with a crisis hotline that is run by our campus counseling center. Students in this class learn about the varying issues that surround psychological crises, and they play an important role in helping the counseling center run this important part of their operations.

# Case Study: The Talmadge Mentoring Program at Western Oregon University

In 1999, I was a faculty member in the psychology department at Western Oregon University. One of the roles I had in that position was serving as the advisor to the department's chapter of Psi Chi, which is the national honor society in psychology. There was a strong group of students that I was fortunate to work with in this capacity. One of the initiatives that the students brought to my attention related to the idea of a possible mentoring program connected with a local middle school (the Talmadge Middle School). Apparently, the principal of that school had previously reached out to some of the students about this idea. We invited the principal to a meeting to discuss a plan. The basic idea was that there was a high proportion of students at the school who seemed like they could use some mentoring and guidance, and at the university, we had a high proportion of bright psychology students who were interested in making a difference. It seemed like we had a good foundation for a program. In 1999, we started a pilot program with a small number of college students being matched with middle school students, with outings and other meetings planned once a week. I was strongly involved with the program at this stage, including participating in two group hikes that included all members of the program. It was pretty great.

I'm glad to say that this program is still going strong (under the faculty leadership of my good friend Professor Chehalis Strapp). This program is now integrated into the curriculum as an actual course that goes across two academic terms (PSY 410 and PSY 411, Mentoring I and Mentoring II, respectively). Students who take this class and participate in the internship experience obtain eight credits for their participation. They have to pass criminal background checks and interviews that focus on their motivation for wanting to serve in this capacity. Each college student in the program is matched with a specific middle schooler. The students in the program qualify based on certain background features, such as coming from impoverished conditions or as coming from an unstable family background. The student interns meet with the middle schoolers regularly across two academic terms. And they meet as a group, with the instructor, once a week, largely to touch base and share about their experiences.

Students in this program regularly report that the experience is highly rewarding. And, as is true of students who succeed in internship capacities writ large, students in this program have a strong record of success when it comes to applying to graduate programs and jobs. And, importantly, assessments of the program have shown that the middle schoolers who participate show all kinds of positive outcomes.

# Making Your Internship a Priority

As you can see by the examples discussed to this point, internships have the capacity to be rich learning experiences for students, often with positive impacts on the broader community. These are the kinds of experiences that graduate programs and employers, not surprisingly, often look for in selecting applicants.

For these reasons, institutions of higher learning have become keenly interested in cultivating strong internship opportunities across academic fields. Schools now, in fact, often hire staff who are dedicated as internship coordinators. Further, schools often have scholarships or other funding opportunities designed to help students secure good internships.

In this climate, when internships are emphasized by potential graduate schools and employers and are being supported strongly by universities and colleges, it seems to me that a student interested in ensuring his or her success should really go out of his or her way to secure at least one internship opportunity during college.

# Benefits of the Internship Experience

Internship experiences, much like extracurricular research experiences, have a broad array of benefits for students. A sample of these benefits is as follows:

- Internship opportunities provide students with firsthand experience in an actual professional setting.
- Internships provide firsthand involvement regarding the workplace, including experiences related to such issues as interpersonal relationships at work, working under a supervisor, and time management in a work context, for example.
- These experiences allow students to test different career paths.
- These experiences provide opportunities for students to contribute positively to the broader community.
- Connections made during internship experiences may lead to future paths, such as securing a job at a future point with the agency that served as the site for the internship.
- Internships experiences look good on resumes for graduate school and jobs.

# The Bottom Line

Your college years are a special time in your life. I see these years as the bridge between childhood and adulthood. And people who work in higher education are strongly invested in making this transition as rich and successful as possible. Toward that end, we work to provide opportunities above and beyond the classroom to provide experiences that will give students every possible advantage for moving forward. Internship opportunities offer exactly the kinds of rich experiences that allow a student to really explore an area in a meaningful way while providing support for the community at the same time. Universities and colleges emphasize internships across academic areas. If you want to be that student who stands out—and the one who makes a difference—you should definitely seek out internship opportunities during your academic experience.

# Thinking About Careers and Graduate School

11

Most careers related to any aspect of psychology will require advanced graduate training including either a master's degree or a doctoral degree. Master's degrees usually take between 2 and 3 years to complete. Doctoral degrees usually take between 5 and 7 years to complete. Some students worry about this time commitment, thinking that they really want to sort of get started with their lives. If this is how you're feeling, I say this: First, note that the need for graduate training is pretty much becoming the norm across the board in professional fields these days. Second, if my own graduate school experience is at all representative, I can tell you that graduate school is an extraordinary life experience and that, if done right, should not be too expensive. Further, it should be well worth your time in terms of both the rich experiences that you will have as well as the skills that you will acquire for your future.

A common theme that professors tend to see among undergraduate psychology students is that students often do not have a good idea of the breadth of the field of psychology. This same theme, discussed throughout this book, applies to graduate school application and an understanding of psychology-related careers as well.

When it comes to graduate programs, it is common for a psychology undergraduate student to simply want to go to "graduate school" after college. And when it comes to careers, it is common for a psychology undergraduate

http://dx.doi.org/10.1037/0000127-011
*Own Your Psychology Major! A Guide to Student Success,* by G. Geher

student to simply want to work as a "psychologist" at some future point. In fact, there are multiple kinds of graduate programs that a student might apply to and there are multiple kinds of career paths that someone interested in psychology might enter into. The subsequent sections of this chapter are dedicated to helping illuminate these areas.

# The Many Faces of Graduate Study Related to Psychology

There are many kinds of graduate programs related to psychology. Figuring out which programs to apply to is strongly connected to figuring out what kind of career path you are interested in moving toward. Consistent with the basic-versus-applied theme in this book, a major way to organize fields of graduate study is along the lines of basic research programs versus various kinds of applied programs.

## RESEARCH-FOCUSED GRADUATE PROGRAMS

Graduate programs related to research are basic programs. They do not focus on any specific applied area of psychology. The point of these programs is to provide students advanced skills in conducting research in a specialized area. Following is a representative sample of the kinds of research programs that are available.

- *Master's programs in general or research psychology* (focusing on basic research skills and statistics, usually requiring an empirical thesis). These programs often include some kind of limited funding opportunities. A primary function of these programs is to help set students up to get into PhD programs. Some graduates of these programs also directly obtain careers related to research.
- *Doctor of Philosophy (PhD) programs in psychology* (focusing on advanced research skills and statistics, a focus on a specialized area of study, and usually requiring a master's thesis and a doctoral dissertation). Importantly, PhD programs are offered in various subspecialty areas, including
  - developmental psychology,
  - cognitive psychology,
  - evolutionary psychology,
  - neuroscience,
  - animal behavior,
  - personality,
  - perception,
  - psycholinguistics, and
  - cross-cultural psychology.

PhD programs in psychology largely are training students for careers in academia, to work as professors. However, many individuals who obtain PhDs in psychology go on to careers in other industries such as publishing, public health, and government.

# APPLIED-FOCUSED GRADUATE PROGRAMS

At the undergraduate level, a high proportion of students have interests in applied areas, such as mental health counseling. Following is a list of programs that relate to the various applied areas that psychology students might be interested in pursuing.

- *PhD programs in clinical or counseling psychology.* These programs include a combination of advanced research and advanced internship experiences along with intensive training related to best practices in treating psychopathology. A master's thesis is often included; a doctoral dissertation is included.
- *PsyD programs in clinical or counseling psychology.* These programs focus primarily on the practitioner end of things and do not focus on research. PsyD programs include advanced internship experiences along with intensive training related to best practices in treating psychopathology.
- *Master's in mental health counseling.* These programs are typically practitioner focused, with intensive training in treating psychopathology and multiple internship opportunities.
- *Master's in clinical social work.* These programs are typically practitioner focused, with intensive training in treating psychopathology and multiple internship opportunities. Compared with programs in mental health counseling, there is more of an emphasis on social structures, such as county and state-level resources designed for families in need.
- *Master's in school counseling.* These programs are practitioner focused, training students for careers in school counseling. The programs include intensive training regarding counseling techniques along with multiple internship experiences.
- *Master's in school psychology.* These programs are practitioner focused, training students for careers in school psychology, which differs from school counseling in a number of ways. School psychologists focus more on testing students and writing reports than do school counselors. Advanced coursework in psychological assessment and intensive internship experiences are included.
- *PhD in industrial–organizational psychology.* These programs teach students about applications of psychology in the world of business. They include a combination of advanced research along with internship experiences. A master's degree might be included; a doctoral dissertation is included.
- *Master's in industrial–organizational psychology.* These programs include a combination of research and practitioner-based education. A master's thesis might be included. Internship experiences are typically included.

Importantly, this list is not exhaustive. Further, many psychology students end up obtaining graduate or professional degrees in areas that are not directly related to psychology, such as degrees in law, medicine, occupational therapy, or physical therapy. There is an enormous world of opportunity out there when it comes to graduate education that follows from a psychology degree.

# The Many Faces of Careers Related to Psychology

The career paths that follow from a psychology degree are as varied as the graduate programs that follow from the degree. Following is a brief list of careers that typically follow from an education in psychology.

- *Mental health counselor.* A master's and a license are required; counseling is provided to a range of individuals with a range of conditions, varying from everyday stressors to major mental illnesses. Mental health counselors work in private practice or as a member of a team in an agency.
- *Licensed clinical social worker.* A master's and a license are required; counseling is provided to individuals from a broad range of backgrounds with a broad range of conditions; working in private practice or with an agency, often a government agency.
- *School counselor.* A master's is required; counseling is done within a school setting. School counselors help students think about their academic and career goals. They also provide counseling to students in distress.
- *School psychologist.* A master's and a license are required; a school psychologist works with the school administration to provide assessments for students and to work with teams to develop plans for helping individual students, often with special needs.
- *Clinical or counseling psychologist.* A PhD is usually required, and a license is required; this type of psychologist works in a variety of settings providing counseling, therapy, and support to a broad range of individuals who are experiencing a variety of psychological issues. Typically, clinical or counseling psychologists are employed either in private practice or as part of a team in an agency.
- *Psychiatrist.* A Doctor of Medicine (MD) is required; psychiatrists work in a field that sits at the interface of psychology and medicine. They may provide therapy in the form of counseling or psychopharmacology; they work with individuals with a variety of mental health conditions, and they may work in private practice or as part of a team at an agency.
- *Human resources officer.* A master's is typically required; the degree is often in industrial/organizational psychology. Human resources officers work for various large businesses and organizations by helping with all aspects of personnel, including hiring, workplace training, and the like.
- *Researcher.* A master's is typically required. This vague professional category is designed to capture various kinds of research positions that might follow from a strong psychology education. Researchers with psychology backgrounds are often employed by offices of institutional research at universities, departments of education at the federal, state, or county levels, departments of health at the federal, state, or county levels, and in other kinds of organizations where research skills are needed.

- *Psychology professor.* A PhD is required. Psychology professors teach and conduct research in psychology. They also engage in service at various levels and mentor students in a variety of ways. They work in college and universities across the nation.

As is the case with the list of the kinds of graduate programs in the prior section, this list is incomplete. People with degrees in psychology go on to a broad variety of career paths, including some that do not require an advanced degree (see the resources listed in Table 11.1 for more information). Psychology is a remarkably versatile major that way.

Importantly, not all psychology graduates go on to graduate study. And although a good proportion of careers related to the psychology major require some level of advanced, graduate-level education, students who graduate with bachelor's degrees in psychology regularly enter the workforce in all kinds of fields. Given the broad nature of the psychology education, psychology graduates are often prepared for entry-level positions in fields related to human resources, educational research, health research, marketing, business analytics, social work, and direct care. Note that those with a bachelor's degree only might have limited opportunities in such fields. For instance, someone with only a bachelor's degree might work as a case worker in a department of social work but would not be able to conduct therapy or work as a full-blown social worker in this context. This said, as explicated here, there are many industries out there that need entry-level workers who have the kinds of quantitative, analytical,

## TABLE 11.1

**Resources Related to Graduate Study in Psychology**

| Resource | Brief description |
| --- | --- |
| The American Psychological Association's *Graduate Study in Psychology* (book) | Comprehensive guide to graduate programs in psychology in North America |
| Drew Appleby's *An Online Career Exploration Source for Psychology Majors* https://www.apa.org/ed/precollege/ psn/2015/09/psychology-majors.aspx | Website that covers numerous careers and distinguishes between those for which a bachelor's degree is sufficient and those that require advanced degrees |
| *Eye on Psi Chi* | Quarterly magazine of Psi Chi, the national honor society in psychology Regularly includes articles on graduate programs and careers |
| Academic journals: *Scholarship of Teaching and Learning in Psychology* and *Teaching of Psychology* | Both of these journals regularly publish articles about research on career-related issues for bachelor's degree graduates |
| American Psychological Association Center for Workforce Studies website: http:// www.apa.org/workforce/data-tools/ careers-psychology.aspx | Comprehensive website with information on careers related to psychology |

*Note.* Although this list is limited, it includes some of the most well-researched and authoritative resources designed to help guide psychology students in their planning for graduate programs and careers.

research, and applied skills that comprise the nuts and bolts of an undergraduate psychology program. So while graduate study is in the cards for many psychology majors, other paths exist as well.

# Guidance for Applying to Graduate Programs Related to Psychology

The following points of guidance are designed to help psychology students find the right graduate program.

*Realize that graduate programs that typically take in students with undergraduate psychology degrees come in all different shapes and sizes.* First, figure out your long-term goals. As already described, there are many kinds of graduate programs and careers that follow from a psychology education and having a sense of what you want to do in the long term will help you at this stage. Do you want to work in one of the various applied fields described earlier in the chapter? Do you want to conduct research? If so, are you interested in a particular area of research?

*Realize that getting into graduate school is competitive, but programs vary considerably in terms of how competitive they are.* Many PhD programs accept less than 10% of applicants, whereas MA programs in some applied fields (such as school counseling) accept a considerably higher proportion of applicants. Do your research and know the numbers. You should know the acceptance rate of each program, the minimal requirements (in terms of grade point average [GPA] and graduate record examination [GRE] scores, etc.), and the specifics regarding how to apply (including the deadlines). This information is not hard to obtain. Create a spreadsheet with the different programs that you want to apply to, including the name of the school, contact person for the program, percent of students accepted the previous year, minimal GPA for admission, and minimal GRE score (if required) for admission.

*Realize that most PhD programs include a master's degree as part of the deal.* Many students don't realize this. There are implications. First off, don't apply to a program with just a master's degree thinking that you need to complete your master's before your PhD; it doesn't really work that way. Most good PhD programs accept most students right out of their undergraduate programs. If you have what it takes to get into a PhD program off the bat, you should go for it!

Another implication is this: You should not expect that work done in a master's program at one school will transfer to another school. You may get a master's degree at Schmedly College and then get into a PhD program at Generic U. There's a good chance that the folks at Generic U will not allow your master's thesis or your prior classes to count toward their PhD. These decisions are likely done on a case-by-case basis, and their resolutions are often less student-friendly than applicants realize. The transfer process at this level is much trickier than the transferring of classes from one undergraduate degree to another. Don't enter one graduate program with plans to transfer credits or work from that program to another program. It probably won't work out exactly how you expect.

*Own* Graduate Study in Psychology, *published by the American Psychological Association (2019).* This book has all of the information you'll need to apply to every single program in the United States and Canada. For instance, it has deadlines, minimal GPA and GRE scores, and information on how many people applied last year and how many were accepted. It also has information on financial assistance. Some programs waive tuition for all students and pay them to be in their program.

There are other easily accessible books and resources out there that summarize this kind of information for other kinds of programs. For example, if you are interested in social work, there's a book for that. If you are interested in medical schools, there's a book for that too.

The reason you want to get the book is that it provides an objective summary of all of the relevant information about most programs. If you visit the websites of various programs, you will find yourself looking at advertisements for the programs. Don't be fooled. I know this might sound outdated in this day and age, but you really should get the book. (And check out Table 11.1 for list of additional resources to help with the process.)

*Give yourself a fighting chance.* As with applying to undergraduate programs, you should apply to some programs that seem like a reach but that are possible. Apply to several that seem to match your grades, GRE, and so forth, and apply to a few safety schools. I suggest you apply to about 10 or so programs using this strategy. I've seen too many good students get shut out because they only applied to one or two programs.

Here is an example: Suppose you want to get a PhD in social psychology. You have a 3.6 cumulative GPA and a 3.7 in your major. Further, your combined quantitative and verbal GRE scores are above the 75% mark. You've done research that was published with some professors, and you're listed as one of the authors.

How should you proceed? Well, there are some top-notch PhD programs in social psychology out there, such as the ones at Stanford, Princeton, and Michigan. Should you apply to these programs? Well, if the average GRE of the students who were enrolled last year at these programs was at the 90% mark, you might not bother—a sad but true fact. The great GPA, letters of recommendation, and publication may actually matter less than you'd think. The field at this level is immensely competitive.

Perhaps apply to one top-flight program that is particularly of interest to you, but also apply to several that are more within the range that corresponds to your portfolio. Be sure to apply to a few schools that you should definitely get into (in this case, programs with average GREs that are less than the 75% mark and with average GPAs less than 3.5 or so).

Without a detailed study of the programs of interest based on *Graduate Study in Psychology* (APA, 2019), you're not really in a position to make the judgments needed to do this best. And, whatever you do, do not rely completely on information from the actual websites of the graduate programs of potential interest. These are pretty much all biased and marketed to increase attention and make their programs seems ideal. (And by the way, applying to just one program is almost never a good strategy.)

*Don't worry about costs associated with graduate school.* Most students who get a graduate degree after completing a psychology undergraduate degree either get a master's degree in an applied field (such as social work) that they can use to get a well-paying job in a relatively short amount of time or get a PhD in some research-oriented area of psychology. If you get into a PhD program, life is usually good—such programs typically will have assistantships that often pay most or all tuition or pay students an annual stipend for helping faculty with teaching or research. Stipends run about $21,000 a year these days. You won't be rich, but you won't starve. So, in either case, don't worry about the money. Keep your eyes on your future.

*Keep your professors posted on how you're doing.* It's true! Professors truly do care. We're in a strange profession in which our success is measured by your success, so do be sure to keep in touch. All colleges and universities have offices of alumni relations, and most psychology departments have targeted efforts that focus on staying connected with alumni. The department may feature specific alumni on their webpage, they may have an alumni newsletter that features alumni, they may have a regular speaker series in which alumni come back to speak with current students, and so on.

# Glenn's Suggested Timeline for Applying to Graduate School

Deadlines for applications are often surprisingly early for students. If you want to start graduate school the fall after you graduate from your undergraduate program, you may need to submit applications as early as December of your senior year. If you wait to start the process until spring of your senior year, there's a very good chance that you'll have to postpone the whole graduate school thing for a year.

On a related note, you should realize that many graduate programs only accept students in the fall. This is especially true for programs that are higher in quality. Waiting to apply to get into a program during the spring is usually not a great plan.

If you want to get into a graduate program in the fall of, for instance, 2022, you need to start your homework way before fall of 2021.

Here's a suggested timeline for applying to programs starting fall 2022:

- Junior year, 2021
  A. Spring—Buy *Graduate Study in Psychology* (APA, 2019).
  B. Spring—Figure out what kind of programs you want to apply to.
  C. Spring—Narrow down your list to 20 or so programs; meet with an advisor to discuss, to help you break it down further.
  D. Spring—Take the GRE or make plans to take the test in the fall, at the latest.
  E. Spring—Ask at least three professors if they'd be willing to write letters of recommendations for you. This process often takes longer than you might think.
  F. Summer—Try to get the list of programs down to 10 or so.
  G. Summer—Follow the steps for each program to acquire the application forms and letter of recommendation materials. These forms will likely vary from school to school; however, the website for the forms should be given

in the APA book. Additionally, this book will have the name and contact information for the department chair and/or graduate program coordinator, who will help ensure that you have all the materials you'll need.

- Senior year, fall 2021–spring 2022
  - H. Fall—Take GRE if you haven't already.
  - I. Fall—Write a personal statement (most applications require you to write a statement summarizing your interests and background).
  - J. Fall—Have a professor go over your personal statement with you.
  - K. Fall—Get three professors in your field (psychology) to agree to write letters of recommendation for you. Start asking folks *early* in the fall.
  - L. Fall—Organize materials for the folks writing you letters of recommendations in a way that makes it very easy for them to help you.

Most important:

- Organize the material clearly.
- Provide your letter-writers with all needed information and forms.
- Try to have all materials get to your letter-writers at about the same time. It is difficult to write letters for a student if the forms come via e-mail across a period of 2 weeks.
- Give your letter-writers plenty of time to complete the task.
- Also, don't be afraid to check on your letter-writer. This is your future, so make sure the letters get in the mail on time.
- Anticipate your letter-writer being out of service during academic breaks. Remember, the winter break may be especially long: from about December 10 until January 20 of the next year.
- Spring—Check your mail . . . a lot!

# The Bottom Line

Your time in college is an investment in your future. If you are a psychology major, it is never too early to start coming up with a game plan for your future. Thinking about the kind of graduate program you plan to apply to and the kind of career that you want to work toward is a good thing. And your professors are here to help you. So make sure to stay in touch with your academic advisor about this process, work hard, follow the guidance found here, and you should be well on your way to a successful career in the field!

# Cheat Sheet for Owning Your Psychology Major

12

The field of psychology is many things. It is interesting, complex, and exciting! Majoring in psychology will provide you with an exceptional arsenal of intellectual tools that can be applied throughout your lifetime.

The *APA Guidelines for the Undergraduate Psychology Major* (American Psychological Association, 2013) focuses on five broad goals that have been discussed throughout this book. To recap, they are as follows:

1. Knowledge Base
2. Scientific Inquiry and Critical Thinking
3. Ethical and Social Responsibility in a Diverse World
4. Communication
5. Professional Development

And as you likely recall, each of these broad goals has several learning outcomes that you will find embedded in your curricular and extracurricular experiences as a psychology major. When I am working with students, I always make sure to remind them to think of the broader goals they are working on, regardless of what it is that they are doing in any specific instance. Keeping your eye on the prize is a critical skill that will help you take action toward success in your future.

http://dx.doi.org/10.1037/0000127-012
*Own Your Psychology Major! A Guide to Student Success*, by G. Geher

So when you are learning about the nuts and bolts of the process of neural transmission in your cognitive neuroscience class, remember how important it is to build your *knowledge base* in psychology. And when you are learning about the details of how to compute a one-way ANOVA (analysis of variance) in your statistics class, remember that you are building your skills related to *scientific inquiry and critical thinking*. And while you are completing that tedious form on the ethics of your research for your school's Institutional Review Board, remember that you are developing important experiences related to *ethical and social responsibility in a diverse world*. When you are reading your professor's extensive and barely legible feedback on your research paper that you have to redo, remind yourself that you are developing your *communication* skills. And when you are catching up on those dreaded journal entries in your internship class late at night, don't forget that you are working toward the goal of *professional development*.

The psychology curriculum is what it is for a reason. Today's practitioners and researchers want to make sure that you enter the field prepared—ready to contribute, ready to be a leader, and ready to push the field itself to the next level.

# Ten Things Your Psychology Professors Want You to Know

As a capstone to this book, I present here, in classic reverse-order top-10 style, a list of 10 things that your psychology professors want you to know. These are concepts that, for the most part, psychology professors try to cultivate in their students year after year. Think of these as 10 takeaway messages from this book.

10. *Psychology is huge.* The field includes any areas of study that pertain to behavioral or mental processes, across species. Topics studied by psychologists are diverse, addressing, for instance, how babies perceive faces, how dogs learn to avoid adverse outcomes, how seemingly small situations can lead to major behavioral outcomes in adults, how people remember lists, and more. Much more. When you tell people that you study psychology, prepare to educate them also about your specific area and topic.

9. *Applied psychology is more than therapy.* First-year college students studying psychology often think that all psychologists are applied psychologists (for example, that all psychologists work to help people solve problems) and that all applied psychologists are therapists. A lot of your friends and family members may think this too, if they haven't had much direct contact with psychologists. Many people conjure up the image of a therapy couch at the first mention of psychology—your prospective employers may even do this. But you know, that image is hardly accurate. Applied psychologists come in all shapes and sizes. Some applied psychologists are therapists (such as clinical psychologists, mental health counselors, school counselors, and the like), while some help organizations optimize working conditions (industrial/ organizational psychologists), and others work in the health industry to help people cope with life-changing conditions such as cancer (health psychologists)—and more! There are dozens, if not hundreds, of career paths in psychology.

8. *A good education (in anything, but especially psychology) extends beyond the classroom.* If you want the most out of your time in college, make sure that you seek out a holistic education. Do your class assignments, of course. But also participate in organizations such as a psychology club. Go to research talks by experts from within and outside your institution. Organize or attend fun social events like psychology trivia nights, student awards ceremonies, barbecues, and picnics. Become actively involved in scholarly research and internship opportunities. Attend academic conferences, and participate in them. Talk to the speakers. Build a network. Become part of the field that you are so interested in. A good grade point average and high scores on tests are great, but at the end of the day, you are a future leader in the field, and the classroom is only an approximation of what the real world has in store for you.

7. *Psychologists do science.* During your time in the psychology major, you'll develop, in various stages during your undergraduate years, the ability to design and implement a scientific study on some question related to behavior. In a typical psychology major, you pretty much need to take a course in research methods, where you learn the skills needed to design and implement your own study. We want you to take these skills with you after you graduate! You should be able to formulate a solid research question. You should be able to identify the variables in your study and understand how you are measuring them. You should be able to design a survey that can lead to easily quantifiable data. And you should be able to compute statistics to make heads or tails of your results. Whatever field you find yourself in when you grow up, these skills will serve you well.

6. *Psychologists produce and analyze a lot of numbers, and they can critically evaluate all kinds of statistics.* If your statistics class within the psychology major makes you feel like you're going to the dentist, form a study group for support or try to find ways you can reward yourself for getting through it. You need statistical skills, so you might as well do something, anything, to make learning them at least bearable, and even fun! Understanding statistics at a basic level will benefit you throughout your life. It will help you make sense of data presented by others and sniff out hidden agendas they may be trying to put over on you. It will help you critically evaluate the news on a daily basis. It will help you think about how to best ask and answer questions you have about pretty much anything. From the fields of education to law to medicine, understanding statistics will help you better frame and answer questions relevant to your work and to your life.

5. *Psychology is not just about humans.* Alongside philosophy and the natural sciences, psychology offers another path to the realization that humans are strongly connected to other forms of life. Not everyone realizes it, but psychology covers other species besides humans. B. F. Skinner, one of the most famous psychologists in the history of the field, studied only rats and pigeons. Many psychologists, such as Gordon Gallup, have extensively studied nonhuman primates. Psychologists have studied dogs, cats, crickets, birds, and more. Psychology is the scientific study of behavior, very broadly defined. We are importantly connected to the entirety of life, and many rules that govern behavior cut across species. This is a beautiful thing.

4. *Psychologists look for what all humans share.* In addition to learning how animals and humans are connected to one another, a standard psychology curriculum will also teach you about how humans are connected to other humans. The assumption of human universality underlies much of the field of psychology. In other words, it is assumed that humans are pretty much the same everywhere you go. When you learn, for instance, about long-term memory, you are learning about how human memory works across people in general. When you learn about Piaget's stages of early cognitive development, you are learning about human development across the species. When you are learning about how we process emotion, you are learning about a basic aspect of human psychology that stands true across the globe. This is not to say that cultural norms, experiences, or intersectional identities such as gender and ethnicity are not important (see Points 3 and 2). However, much of psychology either implicitly or explicitly focuses on what we all share when it comes to mind and behavior.

3. *Humans are extremely sensitive to their environments.* Nearly any and all attempts to study the influences of culture on human behavior (e.g., Schmitt, 2005) have led to fruitful outcomes. That is because humans are extremely sensitive to their environments, and culture, which can be seen as a suite of environmental factors that surround a group of people at a given time (including language, religion, art, philosophy, and more), is exactly the kind of environmental factor that profoundly influences how people see the world and how they act. Culture influences such diverse psychological phenomena as emotional reactions, cognitive processes, intimate relationship behavior, and more. Humans are the same all over, to some extent, but groups of people around the world have their own unique ways. Culture matters—a lot!

2. *Each person is an individual.* You'll learn in your psychology major that although all people follow several laws that govern psychological behavioral processes, each individual is unique in terms of (a) his or her genetic makeup, (b) developmental history, and (c) perspective on the world. When you see someone act, it's common to think, "Oh, that person sees the world just as I do," but, in fact, this assumption is often incorrect. Two people looking at the same work of art, or listening to the same speech, for example, often have dramatically different perceptual and emotional responses. Beyond issues of human universality and the impact of culture on behavior, each of us possesses a unique psychology. Understanding this fact about ourselves and others can go a long way toward understanding your social world.

1. *Psychology can help us leave a positive mark on this world.* The future is in our hands, and it is up to us to help build a positive environment for future generations. Work in the field of psychology famously clues us in to both the dark and the bright sides of the human spirit. And it is up to us to apply this work to help make this world a better place.

Consider the following: In the 1960s and '70s, a series of renowned experiments conducted by social psychologists, such as Phil Zimbardo and Stanley Milgram, uncovered some amazing insights regarding what it means to be human. In his classic obedience studies (discussed in Chapter 5), for instance, Milgram (1963) showed that a large proportion of "regular" adults were capable of obeying an actor they believed was a psychological researcher, to the point that they made decisions that seemed to cause major physical pain or death to another participant in the study (also an actor, who was not harmed). Zimbardo conducted several follow-up studies with similar results, finding that "regular people" are all capable of "evil." Although these thoughts are kind of disturbing, they can also be empowering. One implication of these classic studies is this: Evil is not a characteristic of people—rather, it is a characteristic of situations. If we want people to behave in compassionate and cooperative ways, we need to create situations that facilitate such outcomes. And when you see someone in your world whose behavior seems atrocious, step back and think about that person's situation. You might not become besties, but at least you can come to appreciate how that person's behavior is partly a response to situational factors.

Want a great lesson from the field of psychology? How about this: Maybe there are no bad people; instead, maybe there are situations that lead to bad, antisocial, and often atrocious behaviors. It's up to us to use our knowledge of this kind of research to shape the environment positively and to build a brighter world into the future.

# The Bottom Line

The psychology program that you are in is a journey into understanding the human condition. Armed with knowledge of the broad content of psychology as well as the methodological skills that come with the territory, you will soon be on your way to being among the next generation of leaders. It's up to you to own your education and use it to leave a positive mark. After all, you only get one chance. Make it count.

# References

American Psychological Association. (2010). *Publication manual of the American Psychological Association* (6th ed.). Washington, DC: Author.

American Psychological Association. (2013). *APA guidelines for the undergraduate psychology major: Version 2.0.* Retrieved from http://www.apa.org/ed/precollege/undergrad/index.aspx

American Psychological Association. (2017). *Ethical principles of psychologists and code of conduct* (2002, Amended June 1, 2010 and January 1, 2017). Retrieved from http://www.apa.org/ethics/code/index.aspx

American Psychological Association. (2019). *Graduate study in psychology* (2019 ed.). Washington, DC: Author.

Anderson, C. A. (1983). Abstract and concrete data in the conservatism of social theories: When weak data lead to unshakeable beliefs. *Journal of Experimental Social Psychology, 19*, 93–108.

Bandura, A., Barbaranelli, C., Caprara, G. V., & Pastorelli, C. (1996). Multifaceted impact of self-efficacy beliefs on academic functioning. *Child Development, 67*, 1206–1222.

Bauman, K. P., & Geher, G. (2003). We think you agree: The detrimental impact of the false consensus effect on behavior. *Current Psychology: Developmental, Learning, Personality, Social, 21*, 293–318. http://dx.doi.org/10.1007/s12144-002-1020-0

Baumeister, R. F., & Vohs, K. D. (Eds.). (2004). *Handbook of self-regulation: Research, theory, and applications.* New York, NY: Guilford Press.

Bingham, P. M., & Souza, J. (2009). *Death from a distance and the birth of a humane universe.* Lexington, KY: BookSurge.

Bogus, C. T. (1998). The hidden history of the Second Amendment. *U.C. Davis Law Review, 31,* 309.

Bonett, D. G. (2012). Replication-extension studies. *Current Directions in Psychology, 21,* 409–412.

Bronfenbrenner, U. (1977). Toward an experimental ecology of human development. *American Psychologist, 32,* 513–531. http://dx.doi.org/10.1037/0003-066X.32.7.513

Bronfenbrenner, U. (1979). *The ecology of human development.* Cambridge, MA: Harvard University Press.

Clay, R. (2017). Trend report: Psychology is more popular than ever. *Monitor on Psychology, 48,* 44.

Costa, P. T., Jr., & McCrae, R. R. (1985). *The NEO Personality Inventory manual.* Odessa, FL: Psychological Assessment Resources.

Darley, J. M., & Batson, C. D. (1973). From Jerusalem to Jericho: A study of situational and dispositional variables in helping behavior. *Journal of Personality and Social Psychology, 27,* 100–108. http://dx.doi.org/10.1037/h0034449

Davis, S., & Detrow, S. (2017, November 9). A year later, the shock of Trump's win hasn't totally worn off in either party. *Morning Edition* [Radio program]. Washington, DC: National Public Radio. Retrieved from https://www.npr.org/2017/11/09/562307566/a-year-later-the-shock-of-trumps-win-hasn-t-totally-worn-off-in-either-party

Dunbar, R. I. M. (1992). Neocortex size as a constraint on group size in primates. *Journal of Human Evolution, 22,* 469–493. http://dx.doi.org/10.1016/0047-2484(92)90081-J

Ekman, P., & Friesen, W. V. (1986). A new pan-cultural facial expression of emotion. *Motivation and Emotion, 10,* 159–168. http://dx.doi.org/10.1007/BF00992253

Festinger, L., & Carlsmith, J. M. (1959). Cognitive consequences of forced compliance. *Journal of Abnormal and Social Psychology, 58,* 203–210. http://dx.doi.org/10.1037/h0041593

Garcia, J. R., MacKillop, J., Aller, E. L., Merriweather, A. M., Wilson, D. S., & Lum, J. K. (2010). Associations between dopamine D4 receptor gene variation with both infidelity and sexual promiscuity. *PloS ONE.* 5(11):e14162. http://dx.doi.org/10.1371/journal.pone.0014162

Geher, G. (2014). *Evolutionary psychology 101.* New York, NY: Springer.

Geher, G., & Hall, S. (2014). *Straightforward statistics: Understanding the tools of research.* New York, NY: Oxford University Press.

Geher, G., Holler, R., Chapleau, D., Fell, J., Gangemi, B., Gleason, M., . . . Tauber, B. (2017). Using personal genome technology and psychometrics to study the personality of the Neanderthals. *Human Ethology Bulletin, 3,* 34–46. http://dx.doi.org/10.22330/heb/323/034-046

Geher, G., & Wedberg, N. A. (2019). *Positive evolutionary psychology: Darwin's guide to living a richer life.* New York, NY: Oxford University Press.

Gosling, S. D., Rentfrow, P. J., & Swann, W. B., Jr. (2003). A very brief measure of the Big-Five personality domains. *Journal of Research in Personality, 37,* 504–528. http://dx.doi.org/10.1016/S0092-6566(03)00046-1

Greenwald, A. G., Schwartz, D. E., & Jordan, L. K. (1998). Measuring individual differences in implicit cognition: The implicit association test. *Journal of Personality and Social Psychology, 74,* 1464–1480. http://dx.doi.org/10.1037/0022-3514.74.6.1464

Haney, C., Banks, W. C., & Zimbardo, P. G. (1973). Interpersonal dynamics in a simulated prison. *International Journal of Criminology & Penology, 1,* 69–97.

Hart, W., Albarracín, D., Eagly, A. H., Brechan, I., Lindberg, M. J., & Merrill, L. (2009). Feeling validated versus being correct: A meta-analysis of selective exposure to information. *Psychological Bulletin, 135,* 555–588. http://dx.doi.org/10.1037/a0015701

Haslam, A., Oakes, P., Turner, J., & McGarty, C. (1996). Social identity, self-categorization, and the perceived homogeneity of ingroups and outgroups: The interaction between social motivation and cognition. In R. Sorrentino & E. Higgins (Eds.), *Handbook of motivation and cognition: Foundations of social behavior* (pp. 182–222). New York, NY: Guilford Press.

Hofstede, G. (1980). *Culture's consequences: International differences in work-related values.* Beverly Hills, CA: Sage.

Kitayama, S., & Cohen, D. (2010). *Handbook of cultural psychology.* New York, NY: Guilford Press.

Kruger, D. J., Fisher, M. L., Platek, S. M., & Salmon, C. (2012). Survey of evolutionary scholars and students: Perceptions of progress and challenges. *Journal of the Evolutionary Studies Consortium, 4,* 23–51.

Kuhn, T. S. (1962). *The structure of scientific revolutions.* Chicago, IL: University of Chicago Press.

Larsen, R., & Buss, D. M. (2013). *Personality psychology.* New York, NY: McGraw-Hill.

Marcia, J. E. (1966). Development and validation of ego-identity status. *Journal of Personality and Social Psychology, 3,* 551–558. http://dx.doi.org/10.1037/h0023281

Milgram, S. (1963). Behavioral study of obedience. *Journal of Abnormal and Social Psychology, 67,* 371–378. http://dx.doi.org/10.1037/h0040525

Miller, G. F., Tybur, J., & Jordan, B. (2007). Ovulatory cycle effects on tip earnings by lap-dancers: Economic evidence for human estrus? *Evolution and Human Behavior, 28,* 375–381. http://dx.doi.org/10.1016/j.evolhumbehav.2007.06.002

Nickerson, R. S. (1998). Confirmation bias: A ubiquitous phenomenon in many guises. *Review of General Psychology, 2,* 175–220. http://dx.doi.org/10.1037/1089-2680.2.2.175

Nisbett, R. E. (2003). *The geography of thought: How Asians and Westerners think differently, and why.* New York, NY: The Free Press.

Öhman, A., & Mineka, S. (2001). Fears, phobias, and preparedness: Toward an evolved module of fear and fear learning. *Psychological Review, 108,* 483–522. http://dx.doi.org/10.1037/0033-295X.108.3.483

Repacholi, B. M., & Gopnik, A. (1997). Early reasoning about desires: Evidence from 14- and 18-month-olds. *Developmental Psychology, 33,* 12–21. http://dx.doi.org/10.1037/0012-1649.33.1.12

Ross, L. (1977). The intuitive psychologist and his shortcomings: Distortions in the attribution process. In L. Berkowitz (Ed.), *Advances in experimental social psychology* (Vol. 10, pp. 173–220). New York, NY: Academic Press. http://dx.doi.org/10.1016/S0065-2601(08)60357-3

Ross, L., & Nisbett, R. E. (1991). *The person and the situation: Perspectives of social psychology.* New York, NY: McGraw-Hill.

Schmitt, D. P. (2005). Sociosexuality from Argentina to Zimbabwe: A 48-nation study of sex, culture, and strategies of human mating. *Behavioral and Brain Sciences, 28,* 247–311.

Schneider, C. G., & Hersh, R. H. (2005). Fostering personal and social responsibility on college and university campuses. *Liberal Education, 9*(3). Retrieved from https://www.aacu.org/publications-research/periodicals/fostering-personal-and-social-responsibility-college-and

Skinner, B. F. (1981). Selection by consequences. *Science, 213,* 501–504.

Srivastava, K. (2009). Urbanization and mental health. *Industrial Psychiatry Journal, 18,* 75–76.

Stamm, K., Lin, L., & Christidis, P. (2016, June). Datapoint: What do people do with their psychology degrees? *Monitor on Psychology, 47*(6), 12. Retrieved from http://www.apa.org/monitor/2016/06/datapoint.aspx

Sue, D. W., & Sue, D. (2016). *Counseling the culturally diverse: Theory and practice.* Hoboken, NJ: Wiley.

Taylor, S. E., Klein, L. C., Lewis, B. P., Gruenewald, T. L., Gurung, R. A. R., & Updegraff, J. A. (2000). Biobehavioral responses to stress in females: Tend-and-befriend, not fight-or-flight. *Psychological Review, 107,* 411–429. http://dx.doi.org/10.1037/0033-295X.107.3.411

Triandis, H. C. (1995). *Individualism and collectivism.* Boulder, CO: Westview Press.

Vu, L., Tun, W., Sheehy, M., & Nel, D. (2012). Levels and correlates of internalized homophobia among men who have sex with men in Pretoria, South Africa. *AIDS and Behavior, 16,* 717–723. http://dx.doi.org/10.1007/s10461-011-9948-4

Wilson, D. S. (2002). *Darwin's cathedral: Evolution, religion, and the nature of society.* Chicago, IL: University of Chicago Press. http://dx.doi.org/10.7208/chicago/9780226901374.001.0001

Wilson, D. S. (2007). *Evolution for everyone: How Darwin's theory can change the way we think about our lives.* New York, NY: Delacorte Press.

# Index

# About the Author

**Glenn Geher, PhD,** is a professor of psychology and founding director of evolutionary studies at the State University of New York (SUNY) at New Paltz. Dr. Geher has taught several courses at the undergraduate and graduate levels—including statistics, social psychology, and evolutionary psychology—and has won the New Paltz Alumni Association's Distinguished Teacher of the Year Award, along with a Chancellor's Award for both Teaching and Research Excellence from SUNY. He also served as the chair of the Psychology Department at SUNY New Paltz for 8 years. First and foremost, he is a teacher, and his primary goal is to educate and support his students and work to facilitate their success as they develop across their careers.

Dr. Geher's publications generally address two broad themes: the emerging field of positive evolutionary psychology and the state of evolutionary psychology within the landscape of academia. Among his publications are *Evolutionary Psychology 101*; *Measuring Emotional Intelligence*; and *Mating Intelligence: Sex, Relationships, and the Mind's Reproductive System* (coedited with Geoffrey Miller). He is coauthor of *Mating Intelligence Unleashed* (with Scott Barry Kaufman) and *Straightforward Statistics: Understanding the Tools of Research* (with Sara Hall).

Dr. Geher has appeared in such media venues as BBC World Radio, CBS Sunday Morning, Al Jazeera English, HuffPost Live, WAMC/NPR, NPR Wisconsin, AM 770 Calgary, and more. His work has been in *Scientific American Mind*, *Chronicle of Higher Education*, *Inside Higher Ed*, *Nature*, the *New York Times*, the *Washington Post*, and *The Atlantic*, as well as Yahoo News, *Elle*, *Redbook*, *Cosmopolitan*, and *Men's Health*.

Credited as the founder of the NorthEastern Evolutionary Psychology Society, Dr. Geher is well known for his evolution-themed blog for *Psychology Today* ("Darwin's Subterranean World"). He lives in a house in the woods on the fringes of New Paltz, NY, with his wife, Kathy, and their two children, Megan and Andrew, and several pets. They have a lot of fun together! Learn more at http://www.glenngeher.com.